union
new & selected poems

union
new & selected poems
paul summers

STACK
BOOKS

Published 2011 by
Smokestack Books
1 Lake Terrace, Grewelthorpe, Ripon HG4 3BU
e-mail: info@smokestack-books.co.uk
www.smokestack-books.co.uk

union
new & selected poems
Cover image: Ian Stephenson, *Heavy Ochre* (1960)
Author photograph: Keith Pattison

ISBN 978-0-9564175-9-6

Smokestack Books is
represented by Inpress Ltd

Acknowledgements

The poems in this book have previously appeared in the following collections: *The Dream That Days Break Portfolio* (73 degrees & clear), *Cunawabi* (Cunawabi publishing), *Big Bella's Dirty Cafe* (Dogeater), *Three Men On The Metro* (Five Leaves) *home (in 3 bits)*, *The Last Bus* (Iron Press), *The Rat's Mirror* (Lapwing Press), *Beer & Skittles* (Echo Room Press), *Vermeer's Dark Parlour* (Echo Room Press), *140195* (Echo Room Press).

Several have also appeared in the following anthologies: *North by Northeast, The Iron Book of New Humorous Verse, Red Sky at Night, Well Versed, 101 Poems to Keep You Sane, Forward Book of Poetry, City Lighthouse, Magnetic North, Ten Years On, Generation X -In Our Own Words, The Wilds, Revival, In Dark Times, Marrying The Ugly Millionaire, New Hartley Disaster: 150 Years On, Secrets of Sunderland, The Ropes.*

Thanks are also due to the editors of the following publications, where some of these poems first appeared: *Black-Light Engine-Room, The Big Spoon, Blade, The Chancer, Dog, The Echo Room, The Echo Room Yearbook, Envoi, Fire, Foto8, GQ Style, Hard Times, Iron Magazine, The Independent On Sunday, Moodswing, The Morning Star, Other Poetry, Pigeonhole, Planet/Welsh Internationalist, Portmanteau, Sunk Island Review, Wide Skirt.*

The author gratefully acknowledges receipt of Northern Arts Writers' Awards in 1995 and 1998, an Oppenheim/John Downes Award in 1996 and a Northern Writers' Time to Write Award in 2008. Thanks are also due to ACNE for their support of *home (in 3 bits)* and Banks Developments who facilitated the 'blue-sky' placement in which *broken land* was born.

Special thanks to Steve and Kate for permission to use 'Heavy Ochre' by Ian Stephenson on the front cover. For more information please go to: http://www.ianstephenson.net.

Thanks also to Offer Waterman & Co for helping me track down the painting & to Robert Griffiths, the current owner, for so graciously providing us with images.

for ash, ryan & aaron

Contents

broken land

from **the last bus**

north

(home thoughts from abroad)

we are more than sharply contrasting photographs
of massive ships and staithes for coal, more than
crackling films where grimy faced workers are
dwarfed by shadows or omitted by chimneys, more
than foul mouthed men in smoky clubs or well-built
women in a wash-day chorus. we are more than
lessons in post-industrial sociology, more than
just case-studies of dysfunctional community.
we are more than non-speaking extras in
fashionable new gangster movies, more than
sad lyrics in exiles songs. we are more than
the backbone of inglorious empire, or the
stubborn old heart of a dying beast. we are
more than the ghosts of a million histories,
more than legends inscribed in blood, more
than exhibits in some vast museum, or the
unbought remnants of a year-long sale,
we are more than this, but not much more.

the last bus

I   the last bus

one more tedious chorus
of *suck my cocks*
& i'll be back -
back to the bookends,
the balding pebble-dash
of once-home,
to mam asleep,
& dad squinting at the match

II   pompeii

the door will be open.
familiar stairs will greet me;
still a slither of carpeted pyramid,
still the summit of everest,
still a mystery despite all
my subsequent reasoning.
beyond, my pompeii:
a museum of bunk-beds
& scrap-books neatly housed
on formica shelves,
a squadron of airfix planes
so heavy with dust
that they are grounded.

III   silent movie

there will be
no spoken welcomes;
perhaps a patted shoulder,
a general enquiry of mutual well-being,
an offer of alcohol or tea,
but mainly the silence
of expressionless love.
tomorrow he will bury his father.

IV   breakfast

undeterred by the seriousness
of it all, i tease mam about the
instant coffee; i have spent my
lifetime teasing their sensibilities,
made it my duty to talk politics
at every shared meal, bored them
to tears with history's injustice
& the rhetoric of struggle: not once
have i sat here just to eat. always
canvassing for approval, always
the missionary, so rarely the son.

V   eulogy

for three months they had sat like sentries
at the foot of his bed, watched him shrink,
made sense of jumbled words, poured
hundreds of glasses of lucozade,
smiled at him effortlessly when his eyes
opened briefly & at each other when they
closed again. they never missed a day.

VI   taboo

her words were like a sad old song,
each pathetic line choking her.
she spoke about dad, & how
at granda's passing he had uttered
those words: three times he'd said
i love you, his hands climbing his
father's chest like a child wanting
to be carried. it had been an hour
or more before he could see to drive.

VII   history

he had known nothing but outside toilets,
grown accustomed to draughts; thinking
our place posh with its upstairs lav. a relic
of before. he had known the harshness
of strikes, & of begging to the guardians
for a vestige of their charity, he had seen
men crushed like ripe fruit by falls of rock,
been blinded by shift-end light for almost
fifty years, & all this time a dream recurred,
a patchwork of cowboys borrowed from
libraries, of heroes with his face. he had
done without beer for weeks to buy dad's
first bike & was rarely impressed by hardship.
he was generous with his smiles, but never
to my knowledge ever once kissed my grandma:
his spine was bent, his lungs full, each scar he had,
a blue tattoo, & since his retirement he bathed
once a week & shopped nowhere but the co-op
despite mam's constant nagging.

VIII   witness

witness the scarce embrace
of brothers; in doing well,
grown separate. witness
the puzzled heirs to a half built
jerusalem, guilty only of potential.
witness the prophecy of a single
hybrid rose, dedicated to memory,
without perfume or thorns.
witness the past, respectfully
collected at twelve careful paces;
in their parochial eyes, our ring
of blood an ivy league huddle.

IX   prodigals

we are prodigals
too long away
the orphans of nostalgia
all our singular pasts
unspendable currency
we are stranded
& this hearse
the last bus

art lesson

this terrace has taught thousands
their sense of perspective:
in fewer words & with less conceit.
a joy to draw: a simple clutch of lines,
two ups, two downs & with no fancy porticos.
more relevant, more graspable,
more obvious than a shelf of books,
a theatre queue, a field of sheep;
a boulevard of broken dreams.
let them sketch this: this street of ghosts,
& smudge the windows of imperfect pasts.
let them use rulers, & only three colours:
a dirty red, a gloss slate grey,
the carbon black of detail.
let them learn from a wall of clay.
let them watch as it disappears.

if keir hardie were the man on the moon

what would he make of it? we wondered;
looking down, night after serious night,
on the ancient tiles of our street:
just hanging there in the indigo
like a stringless conker,
distant & ownerless &
fingering the cello curve
of his immaculate tash.
he'd be stunned by our quiet world,
perplexed at our lack of shift patterns,
our weekend hangovers, our luxurious carpets,
& he'd notice the chimneys no longer smoked.
he'd see our fitted wardrobes bulge
with fake armani, in tasteful
soft pastels & unbleached linen.
he'd study our satellite dishes,
watch open university programmes
in the dead of night, learn envy
from the billboard ads,
grow hungry for the horsepower
of our nippy five-door peugeots.
just before morning, he'd shift his gaze,
browse the horizons in search of old haunts;
he'd wake up the tramp on the library steps,
inquire on the whereabouts of some lost friend,
& then he'd remember he's the man on the moon
& not know whether to laugh or cry.

faking springtime

for half a year, this city has sworn itself to greyness,
ganged up with the weather to terrorise rheumatics.

at 6.37 this morning though, when he coughed himself awake
there was cloudless blue through the crack in the curtains,

through the crack in his eyelids, & a sparrow,
whistling the theme tune from mission impossible:

yesterday's clothes are heaped like sand dunes,
the legacy of her perfume suggesting flowers.

6.43 a.m., greyness resumed, sparrow silenced,
the helpless sun eclipsed by cloud, the clatter of hail.

while they were sleeping, the damp patch on the ceiling
has grown into a map of the dardanelles.

needlework

she was too desperate for embarrassment,
oblivious to protocol, bumming tabs and
scaring old dears into making donations.
eighteen at tops, and with the same
exhausted eyes my grandma had:
a tell tale sign of needlework in ill-lit rooms.
she shivered in the heat of the summer sun,
told a grey-haired bloke to fuck himself
when he lectured her on manners.
the coins grew wet in the warm of my hand,
as i readied myself for her blank request,
and then, she had gone, like the holy ghost,
transported away to a light-starved room
where she gnawed the damp leather
of a tourniquet, while the man whose
cock she'd have to suck in lieu of cash
was loading up the needle from a medicine spoon.

jesus

yeah yeah padre, i'm sure you were lost!
it's the being found again bit that i'd contest.
don't get me wrong though, i like your style,
anyone who rants to themselves in empty public
forums is okay in my book, and your commitment
your holiness is totally beyond question: more often
than not though when i pass you in the market, all i
see is a wind-up toy, jehovah's automaton, with life-like
limbs, & your steely jaw in perfect time with the dated
sixties soundtrack. no offence like, but i can't help
thinking that you're just the latest model in a long-
running series of action-man disciples, with your
cropped black hair, & the linear stigmata of your
sorry self attention clearly on display between your
wrist & your elbow, & the ugly blue tattoos which
you wear on your neck, saying *MADE IN ENGLAND,*
& *PLEASE CUT HERE,* & the half hidden swastika
which is poking through the strap of your tacky new
digital; all clear enough signs of previous lives to take
a guess your gullibility is really nothing new.

class act

i have made enemies of posh cars,
even stoned them on occasion:
i have discriminated purely on the basis
of o'level passes -
or the slightest interest in horses,
& attended all doctors & lawyers
with an unequivocal hatred.
i have refused cigarettes on the grounds
of southern accent alone,
made it my mission to advocate anger
for my entire social class.
i have lived ignorant of exceptions.
i am vetting you
as we speak.

cowboys

they meet at the king's
every second tuesday:
harmless & oddly cool.
they slide their pints along the bar,
juggle with their shooters,
sporadically they spin their spurs,
oblivious to our giggling.
a jovial posse of milky-bar kids
grown plump & grey
in a low budget remake
of the classic original:
their territory, a fragile set
which cold sea winds
could effortlessly blow away.

proctor

was always ' a sandwich short', but we cut him some slack 'cos
his dad was dead. in our back-street war-games he'd want to be
the germans 'cos it gave him the license to torture little tommy
& shout *zieg heil* at the top of his voice. proctor was the first of
us to commit himself to punk; showed up one day at school
with a sid vicious hairdo & a snappy tartan bum-flap that he'd
made from a kilt. they sent him home with his fingers stinging
& a note to his mam which served no purpose since his mam
couldn't read. once, outside the chippie, after half a can of
cider & a few brisk lungfuls of evostick, he drove his cousin's
moped straight into a lamppost. he spent the next eighteen
months on this scheme or that, at a printers shop on plessey
road, knocking out invites to golf-club dinners, luminous 'sale'
signs in orange & lime, perfecting his knowledge of solvent
based inks. in late 82, & doubtless spurred on by the ITN
coverage of our boys in the falklands proctor joined the para's,
threw a party at the welfare, took a train down south. he came
back the next easter as the perfect young squaddie: the winged
tattoo, the obligatory crimson tee-shirt, his spawny biceps
more clearly defined, & with endless talk of brotherhood when
we saw him in the pub: how his mates called him 'geordie' &
laughed at all his jokes, how the sergeant at the training camp
had said he was 'a natural'. according to the gossip he married
a barmaid he met in northern ireland but no-one's really seen
him since his mother popped her clogs. as far as we know like
he's still in the army. as far as we know he's the chief-of-
fucking-staff. as far as we know he's the next poor bastard to
step on a land mine in the former yugoslavia.

st. gloria's day

it's finally official: the pope has confirmed it in a multi-lingual coda to the good friday mass. the canonisation of gloria gaynor as the patron-saint of battered wives; her motto the latin for *'i will survive'*. it reminds me of this woman i talked to in kwiksave as i queued for tobacco at pre-budget prices. she wore a neat group of crescent scars where he'd planted the gold of his half-sovereign ring squarely on the curve of her blushered left cheek, astoundingly consistent for someone so pissed: more accurate than william tell. she hummed that song as we waited in line, each monotone burst a boast, a prayer.

mr kurtz, he lives

I didn't tell her the half of it, my therapist that is: the episode
with the sparrows & the pinking shears for one, & that time
me & john garrotted davey kelly with his sister's nylon
skipping rope for no other reason than him having a go-kart
& a swath of curly hair; & digging those bear-pit traps to catch
mr. simpson out walking his dog all seems a bit harsh in the
cold light of day, when his only real crime had been keeping
our frisbee when it went in his yard. & the living kites, tommy!
christ on a stick! the living kites that we made of gulls, with
bread & hooks & fishing line! & only now, with the hindsight
of conrad on the A'level course, & the regular screenings of
apocalypse now have we finally acknowledged we were cutting
it fine. at night I thank god that CCTV & those pigs that fly
have come too late to cast me as a candidate for *prisoner cell
block H*.

snob

blyth spartans 4, boston utd 3; & according to my dad, the greatest football moment to occur this side of war. i tell this tale often. tonight it's to a fat bloke who is sat at the bar: he has just 'found' the game like others find god; preferring plato to platini in his previous incarnation: he raves about 'the toon' in commentator-speak, like a blind man with no nose describing a flower, & despite his enthusiasm he gets my goat: he has never played 'three goals in' with a balding tennis ball well after dark, never said 'next goal wins' with a trace of breathless optimism creeping into his voice, or given up his jumper to act as a goalpost; he has never shed tears at the sound of a whistle, or exchanged vulgarities with a bearded centre-forward; he has never timed a volley so fucking sweetly that it busts through the net like an anti-tank missile; or turned to his mates when he knows he's got the winner. & then he sets off on a cantona rant, claiming that eric is a flash in the pan, 'a gallic thug' he dares to say, 'with a modicum of skill'! so with my eyebrows at least, i make my saving tackle, i make a point of making a point that discovery & understanding are completely different things.

contemplating dust

I

it's become sorta legendary in the betting-shop gang, his great
domestic-chore strike of 1995; how micky had read in some
old book of inane facts, that skin & hair formed almost all of
household dust: & having established, through processes of
reason, that bits of her still lived there, despite the dramatic
exit & her assertive statements of closure; that her lips were
strewn on the velour of the three piece, or that molecules of
her perfect neck were clinging like limpets to the harshness of
the carpet. & being a man for the great symbolic gesture, he
had smashed up the hoover in a frenzied luddite fit, made a
small bonfire of dust-pan & brush, of lint-free cloths & *mr.
sheen*. according to his sister, he has never polished since.

II

it was years before they mentioned the asbestos in the walls,
years in which bronchitis had been looked upon calmly,
& nights of sleep rarely lost on the niggling ache of a lung.
today, much slower up hills, & more sceptical of destiny,
a consultant from malaysia held an x-ray to the light-box,
showed her the future mapped on acetate, like a sonar swoop
on a school of fish or a colony of snowflakes descending wet
glass.

III

the walls grow more patient with each coat of paint,
quite confident the rage will go, we'll shout much less,
grow so close as to carve our names in the inch thick dust
which has settled on the lid of the wedding snaps box.

philosophy

d'y'ever have those days tommy? when even sticking on the telly for lunchtime *neighbours* is a bit of an effort? when you guzzle milk instead of tea 'cos you can't be arsed to wait for the kettle? d'y'ever just sit in an armchair for a whole afternoon & think how it felt to be cast as *ironside*? or count up the speckles on a woodchipped wall? sometimes after *casualty* i think i've got cancer, i think that i'm dying, when really i'm just bored.

the hundred years war

even now when winter comes
they huddle in a clique of pints
recalling between bingo lines
bleak paragraphs of angry times.
old archie's in his element
& licking scotch from ancient lips
lists every strike since twenty-six
& every blackleg dead or not
proud testament, he'd not forgot:
& by the time the whisky comes
each horses charge, each copper's fist
each treachery on archie's list
is credited to micky holmes
for scabbing back in eighty four
for shitting at his brother's door
for always being a *sly faced cunt*
now that they'd come to think of it.
the barmaid clinked the tables clear
came close enough to overhear
& in some youthful liberal fit
began to find defence for it:
so mixed into their slurred goodnights
more anger still & threats of fights
how micky holmes had made his bed
& curses that would see him dead
then home to pristine pebble-dash
they'd purchased with their hand-shake cash
to sleep, to sleep perchance to dream
of a hundred years war & a flooded seam

scab

in the name of christ davey!
were you not half tempted yourself?
when only chips & soup for months
had made you shrink, think nothing else
but fear & hate until you slept, when the
face in your shaving glass couldn't
look you in the eye & the kid's lists
for santy were crushed in your pocket
like a secretive betting slip!
did you not think that davey? never once?
did you never wonder how many more rows
that you and sue could stand? how many more
days you'd have to wear the empty slouch
of charity? how long it would be 'til the sharks
came round & you had to take their money?
& how long it would be before the bastards
came back & took the fucking video!
tell me that davey! just tell me fucking that!
at least tell me that! i'm your brother, man!
will you please look up from your pint?

at the bedlington miners' picnic, 1986

don't get me wrong like, i'm not averse to a bit of pageantry:
but this was different, no longer a pageant at all, more like
laughing at spastics, or kicking the walking sticks of frail old
ladies for cheap entertainment. the lodge banners from
disbanded collieries, the union jacks, & the branch secretary
from crofton who had never properly learnt the words for
perennial red flag anthems. if the pegswood band had played
hot jazz that year, instead of hymns, it could have been better,
it could have been fun, it would have been easier to recreate
my parent's tales, of how dad had fallen head over heels with
the pretty miss west sleekburn, who had sported a bikini
against her mother's wishes, & how attlee had boomed his
ferocious words, when labour men still could, & grandma had
sobbed when they knocked out jerusalem completely
convinced that the lyrics were a prophecy.

wash-day

for my mother

four pristine sheets flap their white surrender
& her, humming the chorus of shirley bassey's latest
with three gypsy pegs between her vinyl teeth.

behind her on the cobbles, an orange plastic basket
filled, then filled some more, with schoolboys shirts
& shapeless gas-board overalls, coiled like cables
& steaming like entrails in an open wound.

i watched her at the sink, teasing out dirt,
pounding a gravy stain into submission,
wrestling a bedspread made heavier with water;

& then, the wringing out, her face contorted,
a salt-burnt trawler-man hauling in his catch,
as if in that second her mottled veins would burst.

each towel, each blanket, each pair of socks,
like snapping the necks of hapless birds
or twining a rope to use in her escape,

her red knuckles, red bones,
made more arthritic with every load,
& set these days like a budgies claw,
her own silent monument to then, before.

heirloom

they were less concerned, it seems,
with heirlooms than I, leaving instead
their intangible constants as documents
of our lineage: the acrid legacy of a bedtime fag,
the blunt reek of coal tar soap, of fisherman's friends;
the taste of cold & of half dry towels, the high pitched crunch
of shovelled coals, or the snapping fingers of half-charred
sticks, spitting their bubbles like grey-faced consumptives.
there had been a watch-chain, belonging to his father,
which had carried a medallion from a football adventure:
bedlington terriers, 1899, & worn down
where his name was, where he'd doubtlessly rubbed it
when he needed good luck. they sold it to a vulture,
to subsidise a christmas, to buy my dad a clockwork train
that he very rarely played with.

the shadow of chimneys

we danced our infant summers
in the shadow of chimneys
each episode a symphony
of bar-code light, clinging
like hockle to a blackleg's face
painted like legend on
the same bruising cobbles
that shoeless bairns had hopped
& scotched upon in onetimewhen.

we left our mark on the chapel wall
unfinished hearts & *shaz 4 paul*
in dripping gloss we'd filched from dad:
our tributes daubed in darker times
with fuck the state & *mick's a scab*

we stalked the kids at number 12
like golding's boys with savage blood
with skewer spears of penknived birch
for crimes of having gardens

we played our clammy sex-games
on the elderberried wasteground
fingering our hairless forms
perfecting all our rendezvous
until the call for dinner came

we engineered a world of foes
of *japs* & *huns, arapahos*
but fought our wars of sticks & stones
for the tenderness of nurses

we carved ourselves a lost boy's world
entrenched ourselves in no-man's land
set vietcong traps against the old
we dug until our fingers bled

we danced our infant summers
in the shadow of chimneys
each episode a symphony
of bar-code light, clinging
like hockle to a blackleg's face

false memory syndrome

we have grown deluded & confused; like old women
who think their cats are human: learnt to exist as curios,
cheap entertainment for interested liberals with company
cars: trapped like soap stars in our cyclical plots, we churn
out our childhoods like excerpts from potemkin. our
welcome mats are flooded with endless invitations to
posh-nosh dos, & we've grown quite wealthy on the back
of our free lunches; the honorary consul of the great unwashed,
& his beautiful partner in hand-sewn frocks so gloriously
resplendent, simple & honest, & quaintly respectable.
over the aperitifs, they feign excitement at my mother's net curtains
or her ritualistic scrubbing of the sandstone doorstep, & they
stare & smile as we use the wrong fork for the game pate starter,
or look a bit uncomfortable with the chilled tomato soup. at some
stage during the salmon course, it's as though we become the white
haired granddad they never got to meet; & they ask us about the
thirties as if we were there! & what's it really like in a coal
mining town, with the whirr of the cage-wheel always there in the
distance? they go on & on about some great uncle who had once
been a collier in the nottinghamshire coalfield, & we don't mention
the scabbing tradition historically associated with the miners of
that area: perfectly aware that it's not in the script to gloss
their tidy histories or shatter their romanticism:, so we answer
instead their clumsily worded questions on the place of social
realism in the work of d h lawrence, & they nod their heads,
as if they understand, when we talk about the violence in our
patriarchal homes, or our mam's bizarre attraction to the company
of methodists. we'll talk for hours about hardship & bait-boxes,
then the taxi will come & we'll kiss them on their cheeks. & they'll
think to themselves as they wash off the make-up in their marbled
en suite bathrooms, of how lovely we were, & so very very truthful,
& it won't cross their minds until much much later that perhaps
we were pretending, just like them.

easter saturday, 1993

'our billy's home on a weekend leave! your auntie irene rang to let you know. she says him and his da are going up the club for a quick pint and a game of snooker, an' if you're thirsty they'll see you there in an hour.' my mother is a little woman, but she's a mouth like a foghorn. billy's in the army, he's my cousin, well sort of. his mam & dad & my mam & dad have been mates for ages, since school i think & we call them auntie & uncle because we saw more of them than our real aunties and uncles when we were kids. it's all very complicated, if you're not in the know. everybody's got pretend relations in this town, probably because we are all related in some way or another. my brother, who's got a degree and lives in london, says the entire population of this town looks syndromic whatever that means, i presume it's not very flattering. i have never heard him say anything good about our town, even before he went to university. anyhow, i was quite thirsty & i hadn't seen billy for months, so i pulled on a shirt and walked up to the club, stopping off at the garage to get some tabs. billy's dad was also called billy, sort of a dynasty thing that had been going for years, quite confusing but nevertheless. they were already half way through their second pint when i got there, & uncle billy was contemplating a tricky red into the bottom left pocket. luckily, he missed it & was able to go to the bar to get me a pint. i was skint as usual. i had a reputation for being skint & people automatically bought me drinks. not that i was a bum like, i just never had any money, by the time i'd paid mam some board & bought some smokes. billy was doing alright by the looks of it, & was decked out in loads of new gear, trendy stuff, with labels on the outside. he shook my hand & made the usual inquiries about jobs and girlfriends. billy the senior came back from the bar expertly carrying three pints of fed special, some salted nuts, and a packet of porky scratchings. he passed some comment about the length of my sideboards then picked up his cue to restart the game. the game took ages, neither of them was any good, but that wasn't the point really; it meant we could talk without having to make eye contact, this is another tradition in our town.

we talked about football mainly but then i raised the
possibility of billy having to go to bosnia or something and
that set them off in army mode. his dad had been a squaddie
too, and had a royal engineers cap badge proudly tattooed on
his bulging forearm. i looked down at the lapel of my scruffy
israeli army jacket, surveying my collection of cnd and
anarchy badges. they thought i was a commi-puff but never
said anything. billy rattled on for ages about being able to
survive for a week on one black bin bag and a candle, i cracked
some gag about tory mps surviving for fourteen years on one
sainsbury's bag, a pound of satsumas and a 12 inch dildo, and
we all laughed. uncle billy saw my glass was empty and slipped
me a fiver to get the next round in. i knew that i would be the
topic of their conversation as soon as i left the room but that
didn't bother me. their tone would be of sympathy more than
malice; they'd say it was a waste of a good brain and that if
there were jobs to get i'd have one by now. everyone
understood, they weren't all stupid. the main lounge was full
of all the lads in my class at school who hadn't joined the army,
the navy or the raf. they all looked pretty miserable, slumped
over half glasses picking out horses, but every one of them
managed a nodded smile as i walked by en route for the bar.
davey raffle called me over and asked if i was still playing
footie, and we got on talking about the legendary comrades
side of the late eighties, the cup and league double, and my
diving header in the quarter finals. i still dream about that
goal. davey said if i was interested i could come and train with
the waterloo on wednesday nights but i remembered startrek
was on and that the video was knackered, so i made an excuse
and said i'd bear it in mind. he wished me well and returned to
his task of picking out winners. i collected the pints and went
back to the snooker room. the two billys were doubled over in
kinks of laughter, more barrack room stories no doubt. i
looked at their faces as i put down the drinks. there was
something different about their contorted features. they
looked weird, like aliens, sort of syndromic i suppose.
someone had put 'we gotta get outta this place' on the jukebox
in the lounge and it drifted into the room like a stage whisper,
i could hear the ironic laughter of davey raffle and the others
as they joined in with the chorus, obviously thinking the same
thoughts as me. my brother was right, this town is cursed, and
there is no cure.

rant

okay, so hijacking that armoured car at the TA open day was a bit extreme; and proclaiming from the gun turret that the beginning of the end of the bourgeois capitalist state machine was nigh, naive in retrospect, but i was only fourteen, and i get embarrassed too when everybody mentions it at those cosy family get-togethers that we seem to have less and less because you think they always end up being a shouting match. perhaps those awkward blushes were the nearest thing to red tinged solidarity we'll ever have and i appreciate that, you're not the first members of the labour aristocracy to be duped by the hegemonic forces of the dominant ideology and i'm sure you'll not be the last. and even now i appreciate your reasons for only regarding me as a sane mature adult when i partake in those pleasant conversations about patio tubs and hardy perennials in which i make absolutely no reference to the unending class struggle, that's your prerogative. but don't go treating me like some stupid teenage dreamer who's still wearing combat pants in an effort to reincarnate che guevara just because i happen to care about a few things now and again. i'm really beginning to think that passion is an alien concept to this family, not the type of passion you loudly display for placido domingo singing nessun dorma or for 'reasonably' priced australian chardonnay, or sunday shopping trips to asda or ikea, i mean a passion for bigger things, for dreams, ideas, for things that don't have a fucking bar-code. to you, ignorance is bliss when really it is slavery; to you, protest is taboo when really it's essential; to you, apathy is a way of life when really it's disease; to you, change is a threat when really it is promise; to you, these lines are rhetoric when really they're confession; to you, i am a stranger when really i am your son.

february 27th 1978, st. james' park

we all cried, all of us; three generations of self-styled tough
guys, each his own version of the great northern hard-man,
reduced to tears by the dubious decision of a referee from
stoke. me, my dad and granda, just standing there in the
pouring rain, our chests a synchronised heave of unbridled
emotion. the spartans were out, a dream over, beaten in the
replay that should never have been, and we'd never get to
know if arsenal were vulnerable. i had never seen a grown man
cry and rarely have since. even when the dog had popped its
clogs my dad had seemed to shout alot instead, tell us all off
for the slightest thing, and snap at mam for no real reason; he
had never once even looked like a man about to cry, and he'd
loved that dog like an unborn daughter. my granda, on the
other hand, had nearly cracked one new years day, but had
blamed it on cigar smoke blowing back in his eyes and wasted
no time in making his recovery. we had gone round to theirs
for obligatory kisses and bowls of broth, and i had sang them
auld lang syne in a sickly pre-pubescent voice and pranced
about like a performing bear with the mustard hearth rug as
my half-lit stage; and granda's lip had quivered a bit and his
booming voice began to break, then mam cut me short with
her prompt applause, as aware as ever of other people's pain. i,
myself, had cried on occasion, but not lately in public and
never in front of granda; not since i'd turned eleven at any rate.
it was all quite weird in a touching kind of way, the three of us
being honest at the same split second, no shame, no guilt, no
fear of our secret ever getting out; and dad dried my eyes with
the edge of his scarf and squeezed my head against the bulge
of his shoulder: and granda blew his nose on a monographed
hankie and tried very hard to say something comforting, it
came out wrong though, and set us all off in one more chorus
of sobs and sighs, and stoical clichés which demanded no
answers. an old man at the back of the stand was crying too,
and holding a banner saying 'we was robbed', gloriously
unaware that anyone was watching.

italia

it's not easy to remember the ins & outs of it, the exact date, the exact year even, but i imagine it being near christmas in my moments of romanticism: & me being ten or so, but going on thirty as my granda said repeatedly, foolishly believing it the slightest bit comical. they showed up on a saturday, half way through swapshop & sufficiently intriguing to drag me from the telly. they possessed, it seemed, a vanful of gear & a small pink baby wrapped in a paddington quilt. i wasn't backward in coming forward & made swift work of all my introductions; him aurelio, her marjorie & the baby peter, eighteen months, a full set of teeth, & not the slightest bit bother in terms of sleeping. i wasn't slow either to seize on his accent & quickly launched into a few bars of buona sera signorina. then i was gripped by a strange desire to recant all the italian sounding words i knew & before i could do a thing about it, i spouted: spaghetti, ravioli, salami, mussolini, martini, lamborghini, ferrari, lambrusco, capitano, excellento, leonardo, bastardo, etc etc & climaxing with fiat. & he just smiled & patted my head as if i was the village idiot or something. his wife was more impressed & she threw me an apple in lieu of reward, it was warm & bruised & had travelled with them in the front of the van from where-ever. i was under the impression they'd driven from italy that day but it turned out they'd lived in portsmouth for years & her mam & dad lived over the bridge in bedlington station. the exoticism of the whole thing was beginning to fade & i was half tempted to check out the back end of delia's recipe slot, but then he asked me to carry a boxful of pietro's toys, reminding me in the process his name was OH REL EE OH & he was IT-alian not EYE-talian & it was not true about everyone at home being a stinking yellow coward like they're painted in the war films, & how my name was POW LOW & he supported udinese who i hadn't even heard of but didn't let him know that in case he was offended & his village was called santa maria la longa & was in between venezia & trieste & was mainly agricultural & his papa had a small holding, two fields of maize, some rabbits & hens, some grapevines & a pig, that he had a neice about my age called flavia & she was beautiful & clever & he promised to show me her photograph at the earliest opportunity, & perhaps i could write to her as she's learning a little english & then all of a sudden he was my best friend, & i loved his wife like a sister, & his children like my own, & i imagined us sitting on the lido at jesolo sipping campari & dropping sugar cube bombs into tiny espresso cups, & laughing about the day we first met before emma was even born & pietro was uno piccolo bambino, & i'd sacrificed watching delia to help unload the van & how aurelio had thought me mad with my repertoire of words, & how marjorie had given me that smile which i became so accustomed to & how peter had gripped my finger & made me feel big & how i'd seen a string of garlic for the very first time & witnessed coffee not out of a jar. emma is sixteen now, pietro almost twenty, & marjorie died last year of cancer far too long before her time, & me & aurelio, well i visit occasionally & we sip vino & espresso & most other things we can lay our hands on, & somewhere in the confusion of it all, there's a woman smiling & offering us apples, still more impressed than most at my grasp of the language.

hand-me-downs

i was not born with a silver spoon
but did once lick yoghurt from one
in the room of a russian émigré
on the eve of my brother's wedding
& i have known too well
that there is such a thing
as a free lunch despite granda's
limp proverbs suggesting the contrary
& i have grown to value words
& visited art galleries
as if they were zoos
& seen more movement in the lowrys
than the other boys at school
& more truth in most things
than many boys at any school
& i did not mind the hand me downs
though the shoes gave me bunions
& those brown high-waisters
cost me dearly with the girls
& i should never have spied
on sharon thompson taking a bath
in the exciting days of her puberty
but will never regret it
& oranges are not the only fruit
& processed cheddar not the only cheese
but had it not been for the co-op
going upmarket in 1978
i'd never have known
& i have learnt to see beauty
& feel no guilt for its lack of utility
& i have grown to value words
& visited art galleries
as if they were zoos.

first love

it will be approximately 11.35
on a brisk but pleasant mid-october morning
we'll meet in a post office queue
struggling at first to peel away the mask of years
& then we'll smile & say each other's names.
nervous at first we'll go through all the have-you-seens
then i'll suggest coffee, which is all i really do now.
& before long we'll be laughing, listening intently
to partners names & lists of kids
to how they met & what they do
& occasionally there's silence
a dreamy glance of sweet regret
but then it's time to catch a bus
or feed a coin to park & pay.
so we'll agree to keep in touch
then quickly lose the torn receipt
that had our numbers scratched on it.

weeks afterwards you'd find us there
in vain attempts to cheat on fate
grown specialist in queues
for parcel post & passport forms
each alert as foxes & searching for the other
through a wilderness of talking heads.

i have enough stamps now to last me forever
but barely enough of youth to get me out of this bar.

from **home (in 3 bits)**

arrivals

morning affirmed
the clouds retreat

a full grey mile beneath
the antics of a show-off gull
wet slate slumps in whale-backs
exhausted by the weight of sky
the colour of my mother's eyes

the rumbling belly of a land-bound storm
an echo in the canopy of emptying trees
of childish numbers counted in between

& the girl with perfect hands
plucks the first blackberry of the year
arrogant in its ripeness, each jet cell
puffed out like a young squaddie's chest

the turbines are steel flowers
leaning like ski-jumpers into the wind

this is the site of a thousand departures
made misty on the breath of stolen kisses

the turbines are flowers
leaning on the edge of morning

the sky is the colour of my mother's eyes

compassion fatigue

outside & above, sky, the colour of failure
the baby cries, hunger hardening her raw mouth

unwelcome autumn lifts another slate
grey boughs recoil & leaves submit

the old man with the cancer stare
discusses the narrowness of his bed

another lonely magpie perches on the roof
the spiteful sky smiles

jaundiced streetlights bounce off damp tarmac
every puddle an orgy of mercury eels

a baby cries, hunger hardening her raw mouth
& grey boughs recoil

another lonely magpie has perched itself on the roof

real compassion fatigue

good question!
how do i feel?

yesterday, as empty as a house
on the day you move out

things echoed

today, it's like when frankie gets it
on *von ryan's express*

sometimes you need to shout not talk
punch holes in walls, break things

& no offence padre
but you can take your well meaning empathy
& fuck right off

...here's your coat

it's like i'm a bruise
raw & purple
hurting

na, that's not it...

it's like i'm a caterpillar on a leaf
when only the holes are left

from **big bella's dirty cafe**

fossil

an egocentric contemplates coastal erosion

a million years down the track,
a portion, at least, of my petrified
corpse will appear in a cliff face
on the north east coast.

some cute kid, freshly lifted from his dad's
aching shoulders will make the find:
wet his knickers in fright, need months
of counselling just to speak.

i'll be strewn between sticky clay & igneous rock:
my gob open as usual, a little more tanned looking.
preserved, the scientists will later impart,
by high levels of tobacco tar & blended scotch whisky.

my eyes have dissolved, my lips shrunk to nothing
& my hair will need some serious attention:
but i'm smiling, i'm definitely smiling,
it's unshiftable, like a handsome tomcat's
musky legacy.

bird

lunch-time mourners gather,
congealing like storm-cloud
on the wet pavement.
a pigeon, beak bleeding

& broken-winged,
circles like a toreador
in the city's muck.
the man with white hair

steps out from the crowd
& checking around him
for children's eyes,
gently snaps its neck.

school photo

we were deranged looking,
ragged kids in badly fitting blazers,
all skinhead & broken nose,
segued brogues & *jam* badges:
ours will be different:
not one of them called after a saint -
they will dip their rhubarb
into brown sugar.

team-talk

knees blooded & black with clarts: moist
troops in the reek of liniment & smoke:

the gaffa is steaming, hoofing the kit-bag,
eyes shooting daggers at les, the keeper.

four whole minutes of dry-mouth silence,
then tommy explodes: *absolute shite!*

every last one of you is playing like a turd!
& *you les! you're playing worse than shite!*

& us, just slouched, like thirsty leaves,
like heavy corn glimpsing the scythe.

follies

steve, her brother, is *staying neutral*.
he's just here to shift her gear.

he bends his legs, lifts, negotiates
the landing's odd geometry:

& the last straining box of her intricate
follies heads out to the van.

so that's it then? onwards & upwards?
brave new worlds?

i suppose a last minute reconciliation
is out of the question?

a tall order even for them,
those agents of fortune dudes,
whoever the fuck they might be?

oh mother, where art thou

the familiar sulphur of burnt coal
hangs in neat strata

between spotlight glare
& cold tracks

a stuttering tannoy bleats
the 3 a.m. train is late

the wind only
the weight of a child's breath

sickly, laboured,
bemoaning

sparse moonlight
strings a cat's cradle

snaring the legs
of consumptive birch

the bloodshot neon of the hotel sibir
scrawled in reverse

on the chemical workers tenements
each grime etched casement

a pomegranate cell,
a ruby in some despotic crown.

svetlana's vague ghost
sweeps leaves

on lenin road
& sergei weeps

snowmelt congregates
at the refuge collection point

a giant club-foot
in the tarmac's hollow

the night-watchman
at the double glazing factory

steps out from his box
hits the wall of frozen air

his daughters dream in english
his wife in silence

& 4 time zones from here
our daisy has learnt to say no

& the concept of repetition
baths, nappies and creamed root vegetables

all things rebutted
in the space of an hour.

novosibirsk, siberia, 20 april 2004

the butcher's craft

the butcher's wife is beautiful.
irish, i think, from that singing lilt:
hardly surprising he bagged such a catch,
a man with a trade, an ancient craft -
his deft knife skating on the rind,
his stitching immaculate.

later, in their humid bathroom,
he double-checks a lump on her breast,
his strong hands reading the curves,
a tender smile masking fear,
the smell of meat still on his fingers.

shallow water

north stradbroke island, queensland

another fat bream ploughs a lazy furrow, mouthing a barrage
of silent profanity. sinking sun spearing the arc of her flank

every scale, the fresh sheen of shaved pewter. enter right,
the shadow-play shark's deadly geometry slaloming weed,

riding the barrel of an outstretched wave, the distance between us
well-flighted spit & fused in the weld of fear and awe, exhale, incite

the breaking surf to dissipate the blood-scent on my hands, transform
the pasty bow of english legs to mangrove root, the tautness of my spastic

trunk into a trunk. I shaman, shallow water shape-shifter, shark-
whisperer, deceiver of the squalus, order of the lucky bastard, the fool

who fished at amity, at dusk, in water made murky by the mud-crabs'
dance; what privilege this, to meet your killer in a dream and be awake.

the marriage

let's go to *safeway*, she said,
let's get married, said he,
half asking, half telling
& all but drowned out
by the drone of the washer;
& she carried on with the shopping list
& he dreamed about a sunny hill,
a derelict temple, scorched white,
inhabited only by a family of doves:
& she asked if they needed cornflakes,
& he promised his love at the altar
of an unpronounceable goddess,
his entire body beaming with truth.
do you need some more coffee?
she said, & he answered, i do,
with all the life in my heart, i do.

& so they were married
between the cornflakes
& the soap-powder,
her not really knowing
& him knowing too well.

score

my stroll to the shop for milk
had a catchy riff in eight bars
slick & jazzy, incorporating traffic.

heading back to the flat i'm tailed
by a woman pushing a buggy
the baby cries & she looks ominous

i swerve around the post box & into the sun
& the band are ad-libbing now
more upbeat than ever & building to crescendo.

the silence comes as a perfect foil
& my key echoes in the chamber of the lock.
as i hurdle the junk-mail the draught
from the bedroom has the faintest trace of violins.

wake for an unborn child

a drunken harmonica
squeals with glee
& pale ghosts jig.

dark whisky rains
leaping like salmon
from chipped cups.

the tree is blighted,
red spot, mildew
& us childless.

a norse wind enunciates
the dead weight of absence.

let's call it morning

when you pulled on your tights
you looked a picture

leaning on the edge of morning

i mention the beauty of it
& you blush

half hidden now
by the silk of your camisole.

kev

the beautiful woman
on the ashington bus
peels a tangerine
with great dexterity.
perfumes mingle, time moves,
& kev tells the latest
of his new found friends
how he'd once been so hungry
he had eaten a candle,
how according to his nurse
he was 'more unpredictable
than a rabbit with a switch-blade'.
later, at the traffic lights
kev farts, loud & proud;
a stylised homage
to *findus crispy pancakes*,
& the kids at the back
shake with laughter.
the pensioner adjacent
is less convinced,
is scared & disgusted
in the same lined face:
& the beautiful woman
on the ashington bus
who had peeled a tangerine
with great dexterity
smiled like florence nightingale
at some poor bastard
who had lost both his legs
to the roundness of a canon-ball.

plain

over denwick, the sun, a burst yolk
spitting its gilt on slumped wheat
painting sapphires on the magpie's flanks

cold basalt whalebacks on the beach
a lime-washed tern surfing the thermals
& caedmon's portly ghost supping mead

finding philosophy in the movement of dunes
bernicia's surrendered forts, fading cup-stains
herding their summits like busy collies

the stuttering copse whispers a ballad
conjures memories, bruised with dirt:
a father and his boy stop work for bait

watching the stars from a hole in the ground.

glass

all morning sand-pipers
spin and reel in milky fog
rising in a synchronised skip
on the slow lap of the tide.
an old man collects sea-glass;
his shuffle meticulous,
his eyes fixed like eagle's.

he drops each frosted jewel
carefully into a nap-sack.
there are whispers of senility
back at the allotments
& archie's glass hoarded
by the bean-canes like marner's gold.
occasionally, he is static, in reverence –

his bare feet, leather-skinned & salt-white
sinking like picture-hall wurlitzers
into the sand: the ice mosaics
on the rippled floor, the double rainbow
slouched above the harbour, the dead seal
on the drift-line – swelled to a split,
like a fatty sausage too quickly fried.

january song

there, like a cryptic clue to all our dumb histories,
the dog-shit footprints head off into the distance:

& yesterday's hockle has dried like sulphur
on the plateau of a traffic calming ramp.

the wind carries heartbreak, a swirl of chinese whispers,
a symphony of lover's names in the sighing of air-brakes.

of all glimpsed detail in wintertime's ambiguous light
only these are certainties: our skin will grow loose,
our bones melt.

judgement day

it's baking hot. we regret wearing coats.
from the slit top-deck window of a 39 bus
a skinny, ginger kid in a *kappa* tracksuit
shouts *paki cunts* at two old arabs.
the gobful of *pepsi* he spits at them
blows back, narrowly misses our bags.
he mutters sorry when i stare. there is
a crusty glue-sore on his bottom lip, &
his skin is overly pink, like a wax crayon.
his two fat mates obviously think he's cool:
they laugh their tits off at his every move,
taking tokes off the *regal kingsize* they'd
bummed just then from the pipe-cleaner
woman with bleached blonde hair. they
smoke it like a spliff, sucking 'til their
cheeks collapse, & blowing mis-shaped
smoke-rings over our heads. they look
like orang-utans, especially the ginger one.

summer flu

i like my new doctor
he wears tee-shirts
to the surgery
& drives a ford fiesta
he reminds me of my brother
in all his shy confidence
& tries too hard for laughs
when he really doesn't need to
but he smiles with his eyes
& i like that in a man

i have often thought
of my brother as a doctor
healing the rips
between me & my father
& sometimes my mother
once even an uncle
at the birthday of an auntie
when the truth was irresistible
& he took offence

i like my new doctor
his prescription is alternative
when i visited him this morning
with a dose of summer flu
he recommended cheap greek wine
& a handful of nurofen
& then sounding once more
like the brother i rarely see now
he told me to sleep
until i was well

the dinner party

one more mention of the william morris biography, verity
& i'll stick this steak knife through your fucking heart!

did your mammy or your daddy never ever tell you?
that you just don't fuck with deranged anarcho-syndicalists!
especially when they're eating! we're the type of people
who'd have no hesitation in messing with the brake fluid
on your flashy new volvo. oh & let me guess verity,
the next subtle twist in your cosy conversation
will in some way make mention of your of new labour
membership - how the herr blair bunch have brought back
the smile to the gleaming teeth of affluence.

& to think i once fancied you!
licked your calf muscles in sordid dreams!

you've as much charisma as a vacuum flask verity!
& less fucking brains! am i the only one who thinks that?
am i? does no one else feel the urge to kill?

come on verity: the dado rails,
tell us about your dado rails,
just fucking try it!

english breakfast

wrestling the perfume of frying eggs,
a trace of whisky orbits *the sun*.

it is bastille day & the pale sky shrinks.
an ash-tray is slowly filling.

the old man with no fingers remembers
the shriek of the circular saw;

his belligerent jumper straining at the seams,
a leaking prostate dampening his spirits.

he had once had a trial with blackburn rovers.
he is dying of something he cannot spell.

last rites

burying a fiver in my palm, he goes all sage-like,
smiling at the union of our delicate fingers -
there are no pockets on a shroud.
each sparkle of passion in his casual eyes
uneasy lessons for the young to learn:
how a movie can end long before
the credits, how the dying can yearn
for the comfort of soil, of clinging fire.

veterans

okay, so you touched hendrix's
trouser leg at the isle of wight festival.
whoopee-fucking-doo!

the bass player from the uk subs
once gobbed right in my eye: but i'm
not making a song & fucking dance!

& before you even ask, comrade!
i have no interest whatsoever
in seeing your red vinyl copy
of *frampton comes alive!*

drinking with dad

dad's are like bank-managers:
they only understand you
in very brief bursts.
a fragile union.

belching out a bellyful of malt
& yeast, i conceded. *fair play,*
i said, *the model stakanovite*
i am not: but where comrade,
in this thankless town,
have your blisters got you?

uncle charlie goes ingmar bergman

they're the only things that bring me back.
weddings and funerals. mainly funerals.
if i had a quid for every shite co-op buffet
i'd sifted through of late, i could take you
to corsica! one more stale meringue, son,
& i'll give up the ghost myself,
just as a fucking protest!

the last man

i am too sensitive to be a centre-back!
each attack stops my heart like an awkward question,
each panicked call of 'clear it!' like an oncoming car;
& it's hardly surprising that the last man in defence
always looks much older than he actually is.
but the manager is deaf to my cris de coeur,
& reluctant to alter a winning team. he palms me off
with promises & praise, & usually i buy it, with my
appetite for eulogy & my vulnerable condition.

i get butterflies three days before kick-off,
have recurring dreams of underweighted back-passes
& headed own goals! i have become a mindless soldier,
conditioned to defend. i jump obediently at the captain's
noisy words, & dive in selflessly where few would dare.
i trip & kick in the name of victory, sacrifice my
gentleness for the good of the team. & I have grown to
pathologically resent forwards for their complete lack of empathy:

& not just theirs, i hate ours more! i envy their goal tallies
& their penalty shouts, & their misguided wisdom from
the relative safety of the opposition's box. i often imagine
methods of cruel torture for our gobby midfielders or
our egocentric strikers, who speak through their arses,
& only then in words of one syllable. it's not that i'm bitter,
or a serious malcontent, but i wasn't cut out for an unsung role,
& the crap they come out with would have galled a fucking saint.

& however good a tackle is, however spectacular a scissor-kick
clearance, or a sweetly timed lunge to prod away the ball,
it's not a goal, & i'm rarely allowed to raise my arms or salute
the bench, & leap into the crowd to receive their adulation.
i have reconciled myself to inglorious duty, the bitter reality
that coach loads of travelling fans will never sing a chorus of
'one paulie summers'; but i wish they'd understand when they
jeer my hurried slices, or boo my frantic hoofs, that i'm not that
happy to be playing as last man, & i've told the boss repeatedly
that i really am too sensitive.

poppy day

so what about jimmy? shot in the arse with a high velocity air rifle by sniffa's big brother, or little tommy, dowsed with lighter fuel, for a laugh, by pissed-up skins; who even now speaks with a stutter? & the gleaming steel plate that's screwed to my skull, where glen dropped a brick from the top of the bridge in a daring re-enactment of a scene from *zulu*! & poor old robbo, who is no longer with us, squashed by a tankie playing chicken on the lines! or frenchy, who got it nesting for a kestrel's egg on the cold blue pylons! come wet november sundays, come armistice, will anyone remember us, but us?

on quarry moor

as frail light crumbles like dried leaves, like stale bread
the bell-pit crater is patient, a shallow bowl of quiet moss
hoarding its cache of rabbit-shite muggies like inca gold

a manic cloud-crowd flirts as it flits, dirtied & distempered,
a mob of hungry rooks circling harehope's empty barrows
& sheep tracks underscore the shivering lapwing's cat-call,

an ancient shepherd's secret bleats ducking the wind-blast
shell-shocked, tired, the lime-kiln slumps & ruffled lichen
cocks a curious ear to thirsty heather's crackling foot-fall.

as frail light crumbles like dead mortar, like poisoned soil
my father & his children, us, breathe deeply in the saccharin
air of home, of dusk, & build a cairn for ghosts with dirty nails.

the comrades

every season brings change:
more empty seats for overcoats
& greasy caps, to prop up sticks.
their collars grow more loose,
their feet rattle in pristine shoes.

the incredible shrinking men
meet sundays for dominoes:
their fingers grip the ebony,
like brambles on unkempt graves;
they eye the kitty like preying cats,

faces receding to sharpened bone,
the skin of one-time double-chins
hangs paper-thin in breathless flags
& when they laugh, their straining necks
like pelicans remembering storms.

from **Three Men On The Metro**

the beautiful lie

beneath a vaulted arch that's washed
with lime, the flaking skin of passing
time reveals old jo caught in repose.
when the earth is damp & the mould
blooms ripe, a smoking gun appears, an
unlit pipe conjoining with his roaming,
georgian nose, & not unlike pinocchio's,
they say it grows with every pretty lie

we hear or tell, with every leap of faith
we make & every unheard prayer, each
sweet mistake, each conjured hell; it
grows like cancer's cold farewell, the only
spell to counter it the hopeful beat, the
fragile swell of every newborn's fontanel.

ghosts

the boy in the denim suit
gnaws on his knuckles
each chubby digit glazed
with spittle. his grandma
looks like brezhnev
grey and unmoved,
the camber of her sepia eyes
preoccupied with losses.

& sasha mechtatel mourns
the white silence of dacha snow,
imagines ice dendrites melting
on his tongue, his father's smile,
an heirloom glass, a silent toast
infused with ghosts & buffalo grass.

mechtatel – мечтатель – dreamer

sparrows & lovers

easter sun stoops;
makes silver-gilt of birch,
& charcoal shadows
dragged through ragged grass.
they tangle like the arms
of scrapping girls.

an old man carries a sapling,
hands cradling its frail limbs.
this moment contented
in its own sparse company.
stray dogs & ferris wheels,
fat sparrows & quiet lovers.

a host of gentle songs
launched into the blue.

someone else's heaven

the smart-arse pubescent
in a bootleg *slipknot* hoodie
& cossack hat shouts
lazy obscenities at a pair
of pretty girls. they shrink
in unison like startled snails
into the quilted nylon shells
of almost matching anoraks.

there are zeppelins over mordor
dull skies succumbing to blue.
2 lads chase balsa gliders
with their eyes, cricking
their necks for a glimpse
of someone else's heaven.

eucharist

the old couple adjacent have us engrossed
he places *moiva* on her tongue, as if the host,
undaunted by an acrid trace of desiccated piss
each sacrament's anointed with a salty kiss,
& each sets free their ancient lips to reminisce.

tonight we'll give the georgian lamb a miss
& find instead, on page 13, the perfect dish:
a paschal feast, 'a brotherhood of fish'
of gilded carp, of perch & infant pike
impaled upon a blackened spike.

their eyes are fixed on heaven still
though cataracted by the grill
& in their gaping, muted jaws
a frozen accusation thaws.

moiva – мойва – dried and salted capelin

mass

we're drawn like moths, in trance, towards
the spastic dance of votive flames, the opiate
lure of hope, of saccharin, frankincense &
myrrh. the silver island's onion domes seem
near; but dark is dark, & what we fear is not

a fabulist's bear or troll but skinheads pissed
on ethanol, whose bellies burn with want &
hate. the boys who bunked off school to fish
& smoke & whittle sap-soft spears & were
not taught the lexicon of 'wish' or even how

to punctuate the breathless lines of fate. the
sharp-cheeked boys with blooded, egg-yolk
eyes, whose golden carp remains, confined,
within the slick of this black pond, un-caught.

silver island – остров серебряный - a man-made island on
the old Izmailovo Estate (Усадьба Измайлово), home to the
Pokhorovoskiy Cathedral

the taste of nothing

like cerberus tamed
a dog called saturday
licks the bleeding feet
of a dead-eyed mongol
whose soul has drowned
in the taste of nothing.
the pastel, nylon weave
of his laundry bag life
tumescent, like the cheeks
of a rank, bulimic hamster.

& here, where the air is moist
with the breath of our departures
we'll navigate a stoic bow
through sheol's frail legato hum

stigmata

this place not shrine but crypt;
for the ill-taught & ill-equipped.

a mournful claxon broke the news.
the sky, rain-charged, a dusty bruise;

so fathers choked & mothers wept,
while muted, sanguine tendrils crept

to colonise the fallen stones,
anoxic clay & splintered bones.

an honour bed for broken dreams,
an epitaph for unheard screams

& let the wishful bear the scars,
their fingers pricked on thorny stars.

the virgin blood of a komsomol martyr
lyophilized in rusted quartz stigmata.

komsomol – Комсомол – Communist Union of Youth, many of
whom assisted the construction on the Moscow Metro

polonaise

define me today
by what i am not

not by the recalled
but things forgotten

a destiny still plastic
all our histories spastic

a pretty busker plays
oginski's *polonaise*

an avalanche slump
of maudlin notes

descending the curves
of her early pregnancy

held breath in the strings
in the soft knots of matrix.

cabaret

i catch her smiling, eyes half-bowed,
as we discuss the hold of faith (too loud);
from byzantine iconoclasts to soviet kitsch,
the vodka's nudged our volume switch;
we're on a roll, we're in full swing,
it seems there's not a single thing
beyond the big-brained cabaret,
no bull-shit theory we can't convey

& she'll presume we're mad or pissed,
or both, which isn't that far from the truth,
not only that, she's spotted we're devoid
of youth. her smile's dissolved, the moment's
missed, another moscow beauty will go
un-kissed, by us at least. by us at least.

lolita

the train arrives; a band-saw
blade through awkward knots.
it drags a wake of banya heat
infused with musk & engine oil.

shark-eyed & sharp-tongued,
lolita basks in the glare of her
confidence, her sculpted hair
as fragile as her golden youth.

she's got that skin that sheens
like lathe-cut clay. as pure as
safely-sourced Class A's or those
minimalist frangipani bouquets.

the lazy swoop of her sponsor's name is
tattooed on the arc of her shallow breast.

the holy lance

beneath the gilt-less stucco
of another slab of martial art
a legless veteran cuts a patient,
stuttering arc, through other
people's intact limbs. his chariot,
a piano cart, emblazoned with
a sacred heart, our lady
of kazan. one fist propels,
the other steers. longinus,
captain, keeper of the spears.

the non-negotiable terms of fate,
condemned to this, beyond escape;
two spastic stumps made conjugate
with bubble-wrap & gaffer tape.

germinal

beneath this arbat honour bed unmade
the broken skulls & vermeil braid
of gouty *zemstvo* & cossack brave,
of inbred despot & jester knave,

chalky bones & usurped thrones
the overthrown & overblown
dissolving in a marshy broth
the essence of the behemoth.

& when they sank this frozen shaft
the miners & the soldiers laughed
carrion gorged on bourgeois words,
the corpses of imperial birds.

the laughter spread like heinous germs
it seeped, ten full wet fathoms below,
where comrade mole & comrade worm
sipped absinthe in gehinnom's glow

zemstvo – Земство – pre-revolutionary local councils instituted
by Alexander II's quasi-liberal reforms

four winds

four winds blow cold.
a haemorrhage of half-
formed moon will wrap
these scourging clouds
in crimson shrouds.

where lilya & maria had
swooned, the imprint of
an exit wound, a cordite
trace, an end to grace,
an archipelago of blood.

the sword is mightier than
the pen. denial so much
easier than truth. repeat
after me. repeat after we.

the long shadow

the grey square hisses
with the melody of vacuum.
a dilatory crowd ebbs
pursued & proceeded
by a legion of shadows.

& the grass is re-sown,
another winter endured
another dose of hope
procured from ashen
blokes at pavement bars.

all history is here, reflected
in the eyes of a pitiful dog.
christ is risen; indeed he is risen.
christ is risen. & with him the devil.

gossamer

spellbound again. the slow glide
of her measured stride, each low-
heeled footfall incising a wound
through the flushing flesh of rush-
hour huddles. miss armenia's eyes
are bowed, her knitted skirt &
chocolate tights are gripping her
curves like the weight of drizzle.

& then to us, brodyazhki; our gossamer
words sinking in the marsh, our thoughts
wandering like a clan of cursed jews.
last night i dreamed of krylov's dogs
dagger-tongued & bitter of spleen,
stripping the bones of my rhetoric bare.

three toasts

to the humanist, the rationalist,
the third internationalist, their
treatise on superstition revised;
who stroked a chutzpah hound for
luck, even themselves surprised
by the magnet pull of its polished cock.

to all those modern serfs who surf
this continuum of the bearable
to those who still believe the lie
that our pasts remain repairable
to those who find a kind of hope
in the words of that meek parable

to the swan, the crayfish & the pike
who despite received opinion are all alike.

departures

& out of your suffering
we will build mammon.

i try in vain to coax a smile
from the faces of the dead.

garlands for the glorious,
conspicuous & victorious,

each faded tessari petal
the colour of a frozen tear.

this city is a conical adrift
left spinning on the marsh.

today, i see home in the face
of every child, these idle

arms yearning for the dead-
weight of my sleeping boys.

uncollected poems

seeing red

wozzabollocks!

ref ! ref man !
wozzafuck off-side !

thaz nee way a'm off-side there ref !
a'woz still in wor half when ee played the fuckin' baal !
an' that fat rightback woz stannin' on the penalty spot !
ee had t'be playin iz on ref ? y'mustivseen that ?
steviefuckinwonder cuddaseen that !

what d'yi mean man? how cannabee off-side if a'm in me own poxy half ?
howcanna! howcanna? a'm here, he's there, ritchie knocks the baal ower
an' a've just done 'im for pace. tha's nee way a'm off-side !

lizin man, a cudn't give a toss what the linesman did,
ee's one o'their fuckin subs ! it's obvious what he's deein !

aah aye, that's right, fuckin book iz !
that's jist fuckin typical that !
sum fucker meks a stand against injustice
an' the fuckin repressive state apparatus
springs into fuckin action !

i am calmed down man !

hey ref, a've seen some shite decisions like, but this takes the fuckin' biscuit !

aye gan on, yi might as well fuckin send iz off

d'yi knaa what it is ref ?
a' woz brought up to have a profound dislike
for authoritarian types in black uniforms,
& jist for once.... jist for fuckin once !
it wud'a made a pleasant change t'have
a formative years stereotype exploded

on a nice saturday afternoon !
but oh no ! you have to go an' fuckin blow it !

yi ignorant little wank !

aye man ! aye ! i am fuckin going !

beer & skittles

they have their problems too
the folks in the big house
the beautiful people with
perfect dogs & perfect lawns

they argue, i've heard them.
it nearly came to blows once,
in sainsbury's car-park;
all very nasty, brutal even.
at odds over everything:
holiday locations,
investment plans
laura ashley curtains
mange tout or broccoli;
even their children's
extravagant names.

it's not all
beer & skittles.

sometimes it shows:
like a rogue hair
on a bikini line
that you can't help
but notice.

a suicide trilogy

i.m. j.a.b.

I   pilate

text-book execution

river bank
pills
scattered like hail
melting like ambition

one last sigh
your claret eyes
marble

i'd have washed my hands
but the water froze

II   wake

canny spread
i said
she smiled
i squeezed her hand
& then for months
was lost for words

III   midsummer night's dream

everything's going fine,
just me & peter pan
tappy-lapping through never-never,
searching for the final scene
in that obscene dream
always interrupted by morning.

then, there he was, as plain
as the day he took the early bath,
ok, so the wings were an additional extra.

some people would die to see a ghost, i said,
& you go doing your jacob marley on me!
i hate this spooky stuff, you know that

you knew that.

he just grinned.

so is it over then, the suffering?

did you meet the big man?

did you get the nod?

hey moses, catch this one

that's it! i've had it up to here with this carry on! I'm going x directory! all day, every day, prayers, prayers, prayers, please save such & such, please save whatsherface! save yourselves you lazy bastards! i've got better things to do than run around after you! you losers! what d'you think i am anyhow? some sort of public sector miracle worker! well stuff that for a game of soldiers! &! it's time you knew! you're all going to die anyway! & it's got bugger all to do with me! so go on! covet your neighbours wife if you fancy it! steal their video! murder them even, if that'll make you happy! put your left over pesetas on the collection plate! draw those surrealist penises in the hymn books! & take my name in vain as much as you frigging like! I couldn't give a flying fuck! just leave me alone!

oh aye brutus

oh aye brutus, that's right! stick the fucking boot in when i'm down! one minute we're pals, comrades, team-mates! then it's out with the pen-knives & i'm dog-food! well don't think i hadn't noticed you giggling with your new friends, planning trips to the bath-house or who gets macedonia! this new toga is fucking ruined! blood stains! i hadn't even finished my floor show & you're trying the fucking laurel leaves on for size! well that's you of the fucking birthday list! eating grapes! so that's what you're up to! eating fucking grapes! not dead for a fucking day & it's business as usual, sprawled across your chaise-longue, pissed! not a thought for your old mate caesar now eh? incidentally, will you be listing betrayal & fucking treachery in the hobbies section of your cv from now on then? I've always hated march, it never rains but it pours.

joan d'orlean

think what you like shrimp-dick but i'm no fucking nutter! & one more gag about the herb & garlic marinade & you're history! if i could just wriggle out of these chains i'd fucking have you! the whole whole bunch of you! you smarmy english gets! & don't go thinking burning the evidence will solve your problems! it's down in the fucking books boys! there for posterity! joan of arc, one, the entire land armies of britain & burgundy, nil! well that's one up the ring for male superiority! how'd you like that king henry? miffed are you? sick as the proverbial frite? well tough shite matey! i won! cracked your whole fucking posse right off! & you! you with the pointy helmet! who d'you think you are anyhow? setting fire to someone with a direct line to the big man? he'll have your card marked you limey bastard!

judas

for the last time lads, it wasn't my fault! i was only doing what his old, man said! & the kiss! had nothing to do with me! that was ciaphas' little joke! always the man for the irony that one! & it's no consolation right now, but i honestly thought he'd get a caution at the worst! be pleased with the publicity! thank me for it afterwards! how was i supposed to know they'd stick him on the cross? how was i supposed to know he's catch pilate with the toothache! oh aye peter, that's rich coming from you! at least i didn't deny the poor bastard! & you lot are just as bad! full of the forgive & forget shite when it suits you! but what gives now? you make me sick! skulking about all day in your cheese cloth kaftans, all high & fucking mighty! cheer your faces up! you've finally got your logo! & two bank holidays into the bargain!

st. helena

oh go on mon ami just one croissant that's all i'm asking! & some filter coffee perhaps, & a jar of dijon mustard, & a baguette filled to the brim with brie & garlic mayonnaise. ah come on lads i'm an emperor in the name of holy frig! & i'm bored, this island has no night-life, not a single decent bar; i mean a man can only play so much chess! & i miss Josephine! Is it not enough that you confiscated my favourite hat? woe & fucking misery that it should come to this, the conqueror of europe stuck in the house on a friday night counting the patterns in the fucking wallpaper. it's just not on! i hate this place! I hate this place more than i hated the bourbon monarchy! more than spending that winter in russia! more than god hated judas for turning in his son! i just hate it! end of story! i'm starting on a tunnel!

perfect

she'll be dark
& witty
& a few pre-raphaelite curls
wouldn't go amiss
lithesome but soft
young but not too young
old but not old enough
to know
there are a thousand like me
waiting to trap her
she'll whistle in the morning
& have a substantial collection
of soul classics on cd
she'll chase a dream
& think i'm it

free-kick

not now katya
there's a free-kick
on the edge of the box
okay alright okay
i know we need to talk
but surely it can wait
'til the half-time interval

i'm sorry you think that
but i am who i am
warts & all like & if
i really have to choose
i think i'll take the footie
at least i understand the rules
of that particular contest

did you see that save katya
fucking brilliant
here watch the replay
see how quickly he gets to the ball
now that's what i call
reading the game
fucking brilliant man

fucking brilliant

fourtrack

the girls in the window seats are giggling; unsubtle glances gliding along the bar like cowboy bourbons, like skimming stones. today I am old enough to be their fathers. they have noticed my teeth are more yellow than usual. *yeah, yeah man! i've only got two fucking hands!*

manchester pete has snakes in his head. he told me so at the *aftershock* promo. the air is thick with *tommy girl* & *marlboro lights*, i stare at the perfectly sculpted curve of some girl's shoulder, my gob hanging open like marley's ghost, like a busted zip. it is seven weeks since she left.

i am still finding her debris. last night i dreamt about doddsy: one minute we're talking; the next he's miraculously transformed into a giant seagull perched on the armrest of my mother's settee. a big bastard, like an albatross; his chest wide as a car, perfectly still, staring me out.

the A19 runs in front of my granny's old house. i remember once, ages ago, one summer holidays, sitting on her doorstep bored shitless - thinking of how many seconds it would take to just stand up & walk right into the middle of the road. sometimes i think i think too much.

anxious

i had this dream. me & isaac hayes were sharing a cigarette:
each of us taking alternate draws until the smouldery bit
edged up to the filter. then we were sitting in a fur-lined car,
which itself was passing slowly through an automated car-
wash. isaac said something about the hubbell telescope and i
spontaneously combusted. the rest's a bit hazy but i vaguely
remember sigourney weaver weighing in just in time with a
co2 fire extinguisher. i moaned about my third degree burns
then launched into a polemic on the plight of the planet's
ecosystem. sigourney seemed disinterested: i think she called
me a *whining little cunt* & suggested she'd made a serious
mistake in saving the remnants of my *sorry little life*. i thanked
her anyway, & shortly before passing out, i pledged to her my
undying love in a string of rhyming couplets. i remember their
laughter; his the lead vocal, hers the harmony, & the pungent
smell of damp, charred fur: then this terrible image of her &
isaac getting it together through the window of the cadillac.

divorce (in 3 bits)

I   no more i love yous

the unwelcome din of time makes you morning
& me no more a liar than an unwound clock.
this bed, an empty theatre, me the poet,
you the actress, all our words consummate art.

II   armistice

the war is over stop please inform my wife stop

III   wrecked

i can't help but feel like robinson crusoe
returning to the wreck each change of tide
to salvage books & stroke the cat.

i have every faith in our chances of survival
& am perfectly aware that by the end of the chapter
mysterious footprints will appear on the beach

embourgeoisment

some day, & at someone else's expense
i'll call room service at the *ritz*
& sipping my mini diet *coke*
from the fridge in the en-suite corner bar
i'll order tinned peaches & evaporated milk
& two slices of thick cut *mothers pride* on the side
& i'll go on at length expounding the crucial nature
of going easy with the margarine to maximise
porosity & i'll insist, without anger, on the
snappy silver cover things & when the trolley
arrives & they're waiting for a tip, i'll whisper
to them softly, never leave the chip-pan on
unless you're there to watch it.

happy shopper

someday, when my guard is down, i might just *buy now & pay in september*; commit myself for once, shake off the dogma of angry youth, convince myself that property is fun not theft! & why stop there? Instead of buying food when next week's giro comes i'll get some shares in *british gas* or buy a one-time council house with gleaming plastic doors & dodgy, vinyl windows, that will trap me & an as yet unborn child when anarchic teenage arsonists come to make their bid to educate the owner class through their dialogue of action. & i'll probably get a car as well, with a shit-hot stereo & four way speakers the size of east fulham, broadcast my arrival to the world of the living. I might wear suits & paisley ties, buy the *daily mail* on a regular basis, & start calling french people *froggy twats* behind their backs. & germans *krauts*, & i might have a maid & a sweet faced old gardener whose pay i would make insultingly low. I might learn the words to *god save the queen*, or actually enjoy a jane austen novel; that's what scares me when i lie awake at night; the awesome prospect that someday i might.

this joke is not funny any more

pallion, sunderland, tyne & wear

salty fret skates up the wear,
squat, obese, a cataract blur
scaling the bank at *matalan.*

       ghost fingers probe, grubby & cold
       exploring the ring road's subtle curves
       reading the tarmac like imperfect braille.

          on lyndhurst terrace,
          a skinny dog is grinning,
          chasing its tail, a frantic slalom
          through scott's mam's legs.

over by the sarnie van,
a page from a *barney
& friends* picture book
is trapped in the razor wire,
flapping like an injured bird.

          frail light paints rainbows in oily puddles,
          drizzle congregates in perfect pearls
          on lorna's awe-struck face,
          & someone's little hand takes mine,
          sharing the moment, oblivious, but knowing,
          craving communion,
          invading my heart like a cuckoo.
          brief glimpses of heaven
          stolen by the movement of clouds.

       this joke is not funny any more,
       but the seagulls are still laughing.

the fisher king

coochiemudlo, queensland

with every step, the flesh-warm sand shifts itself,
cobbles each landfall a perfect fitting slipper.

it is the last day of winter. the beach only two
from empty: a fisherman & me. him ankle deep

in surf, me neck high in the colour of your eyes.
on his right arm he wears a scar; it is the shape

of a flattened gecko, the colour of stewed rhubarb.
he skewers a flailing soldier crab with a barbed

chrome hook. both of us are smoking, both silent:
a muted union of paper & tobacco, of roaring blood

& echoing breath; each of us waiting
for some big fish to take the bait.

morning

goomoolahara falls, queensland

the sky is an opal, cold resplendence
through a chaos of crystal
& all around, the rolling brook's
polite applause, swoop & plummet
on mute thermals. a scrub turkey struts
his shamanic dance & spokes of frosted
light point the finger at the breakfast mist,
piercing the king fern's skeletal thatch;
like a million polished rapiers thrust into the green,
like every single needle ever lost in a haystack.

overlap

darlington, county durham

pristine light paints elms
      with chemical lime
a dream reflected in bowed glass
      harsh words
& young hearts in heat
      threat & promise suspended
in fragile dusk
      a fox running

sibling rivalry, parts 1 & 2

pop

get your thieving clock
out of my dandelion
& burdock.
i only left it for a minute
& your straw
was in it.

shin-pads

mam reckons he's swapped them
but they're friggin' mine
the sneaky glob of phlegm
the bastard-shitting swine
he's swapped them with his mate
for a jimmy greenhoff sticker
& i'm supposed to stand here
without a bloody flicker
of emotion.

i'll pan the little shit.

surge

shanghai

'when swords are rusty and spades bright, when prisons are
empty and granaries full, when temple-steps are worn by the
footprints of the faithful, and courts of justice are overgrown
with grass, when doctors go on foot, and bakers on
horseback, then the empire is justly governed.'
chinese proverb

the warehouse hisses
like a punctured lung:
that insect buzz of boredom,
the slow exhalation of loss,
the creak of discontent;

a subtle medley prevailing,
never quite drowned out
by the ferric scrape of woks
or blades, the plastic-ivory
clatter of the mahjong tiles.

*

the creek is an orgy of mercury eels;
origami cranes & broken dreams,
a knot of reflections fractured
by the wake of a fat carp's back

*

tonight the moon's face is bloodless & cold.
we drink more rice wine, smoke endless cigarettes,
conjuring the gentleness of the village's eyes.

*

& in the alchemy
of relentless drizzle
this dust has turned
to congealed blood

*

the walls are the colour of silkie eggs:
blistered, violated, flaking like memory.
*

star anise & stale sweat , wet rust & desiccated piss,
all of it eclipsed by the acrid reek of alienation.

*

last night i dreamt of them again:
eight hundred dead heroes.
this slow breeze a keening,
a symphony of posturing cats,
zhou xuan's spectral songs swooping
through these shanghai nights
with the frailty of bats

*

jianyu beats his mattress into submission, seeks out the rarity
of comfort, the broadness of his fist flattening out the storm-
gulley imprint of a heavy limb, the lunar crater of a hip; a
temporary universe of silver dust hangs in the vacuum
melody of the basement caught in the beams of the zhabei's
shrinking light. he has not seen his wife in 14 months.

*

& remember these eyes, defeated & captive,
yearning for the emptiness of arc horizons.

above us, & below, obese clouds, rain-charged,
have taken on the colour of imperfect jade.

*

on people's square
ghost horses stampede;
the clatter of their hooves
like some percussive hymn.

they say the city's crows
grew far too fat to ever fly;
a thoroughbred sacrifice
to a life of concessions.

vampire

romania

I

the birds are like us, they yearn for spring. today, they sound a little agitated, their songs are punctuated with minor notes.

II

when night comes and the shadows start their dance, the demons in my blood awaken; streaming through my veins like a shoal of poisonous fish. by morning, another piece of me has been colonised, another piece of me will belong to them.

III

here, democracy is a child; at best, a gangling adolescent. it takes a longer time to unlearn the old ways than it does to learn new ones.

IV

his dad paid someone he met to connect them to the mains. of course, it's illegal but in the shanties it means real lights, hot water and maybe a satellite tv if you're lucky. poor mihai was just too curious. he had always liked to dismantle things, to see how they worked: toy cars, calculators, the old fridge we found on the rubbish tip, he even cut open a dead rook once just to see. anyhow, he stuck a screwdriver into the connector box and that was it. dead in a second. like being struck by lightning. 30,000 volts fired in to him through the tips of his fingers. his bare feet were too dry to act as an earth and so the electricity stayed in him, whizzed around, cooked him like a blood sausage. when the circuit finally shorted and his dad went to investigate, mihai had already been dead for a minute or so. nicu reckons the out-house smelt of roast pork and burnt hair.

V

the morning of the funeral, the sun rose reluctantly, sanguine, like a giant egg-yolk blighted with a spot of blood. mother is a wreck. i think she might have sworn at the patriarch. I still haven't been able to cry but she hasn't stopped wailing for 32 hours, her eyes have almost imploded, she looks like a zombie. they'll have to do all they can to stop her jumping in the grave with the casket. dad's gone off somewhere; no one has seen him since last night.

VI

the *palinca* has transformed my grandfather into a wise-man. three times in as many minutes he tells us it is important that we do not forgot how to smile. he says smiles are like the sun and rain; without them, nothing can grow.

VII

and death was just another door. nicu placed his brother's stuff carefully into an old *saltza* cracker tin and stashed them next to his new shoes on the bottom shelf of the wardrobe. not much to show for twelve years of life really: a tarnished silver crucifix, a pen-knife, a tatty a5 scrapbook dedicated to gheorghe hagi, a single american dollar, a soviet-type lead soldier, two pieces of pyrite and a small collection of lapwing's feathers. his father still hasn't come home since the funeral. he's on another bender, homebrew vodka and painkillers, the usual. i hope they work.

hammy the hamster's last words

this place smells
like a hamster cage!

can you not even
empty the ash-trays?

the neighbours complain
that i'm keeping them up

with the squeak of my wheel
but what else is there to do?

i haven't got a telly
with an earphone socket!

& i'm sick of seeds
i want some meat!

do you hear me?
i want some meat!

you're always asleep
when i'm wanting to talk

it's like banging your
head against walls!

i'll impale myself
on my water bottle tube.

that'll teach you!
do you hear me?

that'll teach you!

broken land

broken land

delhi surface mine, blagdon, northumberland

arnie stuffs the remnants of an over-ripe
banana into his gob. *"how'd you know
that's a fitter's car?"* rhetorical question.

*"it's had a fucking flat tyre for ten weeks
& he still hasn't got 'round to putting
the cunt right!"* everyone laughs

apart from stobbart. the *cb* crackles
in a distant storm: the air-con is buggered
on the triple 7, cooking dougie's feet

like a sunday roast. at *cut 10*
they're down onto coal. the *dh120*
crawls over to help, stripping

the last two foot of fireclay &
white thill, exposing as it does, the
glint of the *high main's* perfect jet

& brenkley's legacy of linear cuts,
a weave of neat roads, their roofs
collapsed, each groaning strata

subsided, their rolleyways rusted now,
twisted & arthritic, & caught like fossils
in the cold grip of grey shale, a line of

extant tubs, their buckled sides
sucked in like a chain-smoker's
cheeks. deserted & abandoned,

driven out by wet, or worse,
or curse; the past revealing
its faults. & over bait

a litany of *easyjet* jaunts, of
gob-shite wisdom, the patterns
of their frozen words lost

in the fog of steaming tea.
& there's a deer by the lagoons,
proud & still, a statue captured

in the turquoise sheen,
the crackle glaze of reeds
reflected, drawing cross-hairs

on its perfect flank. & two young
hares play *chasey* on the overburden
mound, their fur burnished copper,

every muscle taut as a bow-string.
a thin seam of cloud shimmers
in pale skies & ian's calm eyes

mirrored in the steel of the auger
bit. high on the re-shaped bund
damp earth slumps, a river

of boulder clay tumbling
down the steps & outside
the fitter's cabin, three

generations of feral cats
bask in rare october sun.
the one minute siren squeals

its warning, blunt echoes
ricocheting off the southern wall;
the plant silenced, a neat rank

of bore-holes readying themselves
for the hit. it comes like lightning
over sea. the thud of the *det*

discharged, the ripple of displaced
stone, a shock-wave rising, climbing
your legs like autumn damp.

a brief dance of orange smoke
hanging like genies over the shelf
& the dust will settle, as usual,

the calloused earth split,
the vacuum sigh of separation,
the slow lurch of broken land.

advent

tow law, co. durham

brutal rain this
a rain that hurts
melts windows
& a man's resolve

the dull, wet copper
of a kestrel corpse
punctuates puddles
on inkerman road

blood-spot revelation
pathetic & prophetic
his heart punctured
by a hawthorn spear

& brutal rain this
the end of beauty
leper trees repent
wind-blast & guilt

winter's only hope
an arc halo on the fell
the accusatory finger
of low, cold sun.

anthem

longbenton, north tyneside

beneath the new welcome sign
curiously sponsored by *findus*,
someone has scrawled in
scarlet permanent marker:
abandon hope all ye who enter here.

paddy's *staffie* looks bored,
sniffing the tyres of a *4 x 4*.
it's kicking off outside *spar*.
the lass in a *mckenzies* top
is making her gob go,

griefing some biddy over *nowt*;
white lightning ripping through
the darkness of her bright red head.
& little ryan mimics the call
of a fledgling blackbird,

his heavy eyes fixed on the heavens.
he contemplates the scarcity of gentle words;
how hope and love can flirt with extinction.
& over by the war memorial
a gaggle of *burberry* charvs

take tokes on a badly rolled spliff.
more fragile dreams are shelved,
dissolving in a puff of smoke
the colour of duck eggs
or rain-charged dusk.

bowesfield

stockton-on-tees

cold thornaby amassed on high,
the blank escarpment wilting.

manic clouds paint shadows on the clarts,
the stooping reeds a stop-frame flicker,

red shank & bunting, bittern, tit,
a hatch of damsel-fly drowning

in the mercury of the bottom pond,
pricking its surface with the last of their breath.

a gypsy horse has broken its chains,
only the rusted barbs of wire & gorse

to keep him bound, un-free, enclosed,
locked in, he'll eye his bloodied hock;

two builders from the *wimpey* site, one young,
one old, corral it to the safety of black bobby's field,

high-vis toreadors & tango steps
their riggers gripped in the mire of warm clay.

through bladder sedge & spikey rush
the sorry ghosts of plangent shrikes

lost in the whisper of october's songs,
in the fragile dance of the frail mare's tail.

coda to a snow flurry

cowpen estate, blyth, northumberland

a scattering of brittle white
grips the lip of every slate

daubs stage-paint lights
on the steel of lamp-posts

& i have grown tired waiting
waiting for sepia drifts as high

as the fake fur collar on mam's best coat
as the top-deck window of a northern bus

i have grown tired waiting
more careless with nostalgia

consequence

west sleekburn, northumberland

somewhere here, or near here, my grandda's strong fingers
were lost to the spoil. mid-morning, grey summer, the war
just over. repairing the hydraulics on a self-propelled
conveyor. distraction reaps consequence. four times in as
many minutes; geordie gledson's constant witter: a bus trip to
blackpool, a tip for kempton, a nagging gall-stone & the price
of cheese. a lapse that's all, a split-second too slow, a reflex
dulled & the rest history: a swollen row of badly stitched
stumps, another grim tale for a legion of bairns, the
simplicity of a hand-shake made memorable forever.

drift

north blyth, northumberland

why write of the sun?
it celebrates itself.

over boca chica,
a dirty cloud

becomes a swan
& then, an angel

proud pegasus
by battleship wharf

& gone before
the thatch of staithes

reflected in the mercury
of dormant blyth.

fugue

kirkwhelpington, northumberland

ride on grey horse,
great badger, sky,

paint the gates of heaven
with a day-old bruise;

charge north into this realm
of shrinking days,

find comfort in the welcome
of your mother's swollen tit.

on ferneyrigg
the cairns recoil

beneath their furrowed
skin of blood & soil.

great wanney crag
& black down flow

lay down a basalt
shadow & let the cold

placate the brooding plain
of whinstone & of ling

who's alchemy of opposites
will conjure sobre amethyst

from dour bog cotton's
cataract mist of cuckoo spit

windsong & wingbeat,
a shifting maze of quiet

words, of hymns, of hawthorn trees
bent double in the lisping breeze,

the hollow names of lovers
& the dead; the croft & the byre

the gurgle of a dying fire.
& shivering, the manic stoat

pulls on his winter coat,
in this, a land exposed,

enclosed, exhausted & diseased,
defeated by the thankless clock,

the march of time, the bloody scot,
the reiver hoard, the sundew & the liverwort.

at crookdean & at whelpington
those parch-mark ghosts

from darker times have found
their voice, upset their hosts;

on canny cleugh
& sweethope loughs

their whispers have become a song
a rallying cry to call the throng

of peewit, raven, merlin too
& all those other midnight folk,

the bield hill legion
of whom legend spoke:

& the landfall murmur
of their limbo weary feet

shall be silenced once again
by a fathom of damp peat.

harehope quarry

frosterley, co. durham

dance mizzle ghosts
stumble down these seams

precarious, the tumblers perch
pocked by frost & stung by rain

they mourn their destiny on the shelf.
dun jim & *kit* prop up their bastard twins

each seditious sediment an unread line
every crabby strata a relic, stigmata,

shivering in the kiss of the dale's wet breath;
each heave, each lurch, each fault exposed

admitted to, denied, each mica epoch underscored,
each sill, each fragile schist, the faint arc of moments lost,

the silken memory of their touch, a trace dissolved
& landlocked now, the wholeness of another time

left captured in the turquoise of bernician seas,
bath-warm & gentle. so close your eyes & hear the waves

of history breaking on the sand, historia inviolate, revealed
my dermis, epidermis, flesh, my calcite veins, my heart exposed

each fold of milky quartz a trace of marbled fat
grown mummified within the weight of years,

& shine on now my silica stars, my scars
the ochre stain of blood & ore comes spilling from my face

with the ripeness of confession. & close your eyes
& hear the waves. a legion of pale birch amassed

in ranks that grip the scree with desperate claws
& skirt the icy threats of this dark pool.

the last post sounds his song of shells & dirt,
a million years in waiting to adorn

the altars of a hundred states
& fine estates, to pave the floor of heaven.

& what of him, the foreman in his sunday suit,
hollow man & grey, invisible in prickled light

half-hidden in the lazy weave of shale
concealed 'til just the threat of him remains

like a shadow left behind, the weight
of his being impressed into this moss;

recoiling slowly in these shrinking days.
& what ghosts now will come?

an otter paw insignia on cold clay,
a bloom of mould on last week's dead,

temporarily brilliant in the low sun sheen.
yes, temporary this, but brilliant.

harvest moon

flodden, northumberland

wash spilled blood
flush the fallow land

make rust of rabbit fur
of mica frost & dust of us

a history consumed
lost in the pulse

of the starlings'
breathless dance

& rowdy ghosts have drank
the dew pond dry

cloaked their creaking bones
in ermine dusk & left

a night that's stained
with humbled dreams.

hymn

burradon, north tyneside

reluctantly, the fore-shift lads
rub sleep from squinting eyes.

disjunctive percussion
on toad-back cobbles:

the morse code click
of hob-nail boots,

nipper dodds' shite cart
emptying the middens.

& dust-bruised *shunties*
creak & groan in monotone,

the black lung wheeze
of a north sea breeze

bemoaning her lament
through leafless trees,

the poss-tub drums & clashing
pans, deliveries at *percy hann's*

proclaiming a fanfare
for the common man.

the first frost of winter
is gnawing at our fingers.

we will sing these histories
 like half-forgotten hymns;

all of their meanings
lost in translation.

john innes no. 2

north shields, north tyneside

re-potting the survivors
of last year's geraniums,
we revel in paraffin warmth
marvel at merging clouds
the rare blue of easter sky.

if you concentrate, i'll say,
you can see the algae grow
in emerald peaks on humid glass,
imagine them at pristine dawn
draped in the fur of perfect snow.

the boys will strain their tiny necks
extending up like suckling calves
with every sinew cable tight
they'll nuzzle in the welcome
of my favourite old jumper;

the tired twill infused with oil,
hard-work & riddled soil,
the raisin sweetness
of a hundred smoky pubs;
& to all the world we're lost

amongst plastic terracotta
& number two compost, we're lost
in the promises of another spring
either that, or in wonder at
the majesty of some other thing.

broken

st mary's church, horton, northumberland

we are digging graves for our dreams
a cold tumour of cloud spitting its bridle
throws an obese cherub from its back

thunder succumbing to twisted reason
the ghost-child pockets pearls of frozen dew
fragile grass dissolving to powdered jade

blue moonlight barcodes through the birch
anoxic fingers cupping us in their desperate grip
see the brick shattered by a single night of frost

a concave heaven reflected
in the newness of our spades

matins

inner farne, northumberland

bee-song & bird,
the *haliwerfolc* still

a-bed, fermenting dreams;
so gentle cuthbert preached

his sermon to the seals.
the word let loose

like terns, they scribed
the pewter of this sky

with wings as white
as pristine shrouds.

they called upon the sun
to thaw these carrion days;

enough to glaze our puppy eyes,
to calm an ocean's racing pulse.

plea

cambois, northumberland

a fleet of spectral *deltics* creep
disturb the midnight indigo of sleep.
a fragile coble lost to angry waves,
this sea a field of unmarked graves.

skarv & *freemad's* drowning pleas
each fragile hull aground *green skeer*
norse-man sloops brought to their knees
they show themselves then disappear;

& folly, pitman lifeboat crew
brave sentinels to *brig* & barque
who plucked them from the deadly blue;
those fearless men of rock & dark.

black shadows congregate, console,
like mourners on the furrowed sands,
weep that we have let this gold, this coal
slip through the grip of our weak hands.

& from the grey unwelcome beach
the maudlin curlew's dull lament;
& seagulls will the gale beseech
to heal these bricks, this dead cement.

& crab-pot ribs have formed a cage,
the driftwood pyre too damp to burn;
this history will take us an age
to learn & then, at once, unlearn.

prayer

new hartley, northumberland

lash the salt lick of rain
the gentle sea exhales

a spell, a liturgy compiled
to warm the tears that bowl

across our cheeks. release
us from this bloodline curse

un-snare us from the shadows
of our lead-grey pasts & spew

the truth, let loose those hopeful
words grown tangled in the wind

to help us find an unquenched light
still burning in the sanguine dusk

of every curlew's hymnal. & conjure
all your alchemy to fashion us

the armour of a single heartfelt smile
that we may face on equal terms

the bitter, unrelenting ranks
of memory's ill-tempered hoard.

quench

wolsingham steel-works, co.durham

rich history this, & strong; anchored
in the blood-scent of molten metal.

a century & more of ironstone,
of ore & every toad-back cobble

speaks of air-less toil & rusted pride,
the crucible aglow like rampant sun.

& bessemer's strange alchemy still calls
upon the icy rain to quench its thirst,

to cure these ills, to make this bitter
prophecy in flux, now liquidus.

& the flask will be broken, the last cast
set free, & cheek by cheek, the cope & drag

are pulled apart like scrapping girls; their
final tame reveal the burnish of a cartoon

heart, unsullied by the acne pock of burnt
on sand, but cracked & split in two upon

the fractured fault-line of a tear. attwood,
rogerson, blair & bond, redundant names

here lost & found; steel-men of the dale
look down upon this river's ox-bow turns

& each give out a bellow sigh to fire up
this furnace once again. re-cast this legend

without flaws, re-forge it as a testament,
to all those red-faced men who won

her fame, a legacy to last beyond this lame
farewell: a truly pristine heart in weardale air:

our last steel annealed, a monument, a relic,
a marriage annulled, a death, a fate sealed.

regeneration

sunniside, sunderland, co. durham

on norfolk street
a man who has one shoe
& smells of *special brew*
is speaking in tongues.

oblivious, his form intrudes.
mizzle dances, cold & chill,
the streetscape blurred
in melted pastel aquarelle.

his jaundiced eyes
are poisoned with loss.
he bums a tab from a lad
who looks like matt goss

from *bros*. except fatter.
& platitudes discharged, he
stumbles on foyle street's
toad-back cobbles. every foot-

fall precarious. he catches
a version of his face sneering
back from the windows of
the place. begins his next

soliloquy: how every
disappointment will leave
a scar. how every *stanley*
knife slash will leave a scar.

& how empathy, by far,
the hardest thing
to keep maintained.
& after hours, he'll lie

prostrate, near pristine grass,
his spastic body in an arc.
lifeless perhaps & cold,
black as granite in a sculpted

slump. oblivious his form
intrudes; it grips the pavement
like a half-sucked sweet spilled
from someone's flapping gob.

an ending reflected in the highly
polished chrome of a public art
wish-bone. there's a blood-stain
& some broken glass. neither

are there by morning.

requiescat

wallsend, north tyneside

I

the chimney sweep
has lost his wife.

one minute alive,
the next quite dead;

prone in the co-op
between dental floss

& sanitary-towels.
she smiled in her sleep,

her basket by her side;
half full or half empty

& bringing to mind
a philosopher's glass.

II

a day squat & cold,
shy in its lack of light.

davey downs tools
for a breakfast smoke.

near the incinerator
he studies a crate,

ponders its emptiness,
his wet eyes a plea

his lost soul rescued
by a flash of pale sun,

a memory unlocked,
some curse undone.

reveillez

north shields, north tyneside

somewhere between
the bittersweet kiss
of kick-start ristretto
& lady grey elevenses
we steal an hour in awe
of the painfully simple.

warm air & magic light
drawing the venom
of last night's darkness:
the lime sheen
of newborn laurel,
magnolia buds,

their monroe hips,
a loved-up choir
of hedonist finches,
a fledgling dream
in someone's eye,
a sky that's lapis lazuli.

spoil

east sleekburn, northumberland

two magpies scrap, half-war, half play,
& here, a bed of rainbow dahlias grow
where once a permanence of grey
was forged beneath the long shadow

of chimneys spewing smoke & steam
distended heaps of ash & spoil
conspired, in some apocalyptic dream
well-wrought by pitmen's black-lunged toil.

the march of the landless mice

cramlington, northumberland

witness the march of the landless mice
snaking like some poisoned brook
through all our threatless cul-de-sacs.

toe to tail they'll come, no, nose to tail,
a seamless carpet of rodent grey,
like ancient plagues or refugees,

they'll plot a curve upon a map & plod
into the heartlands of all our rancid artifice.
each barley-field they once possessed

a fresh veneer of concrete or of tar,
the rumble of our 4x4s, the garish
skin of plastic slate & orange brick,

the reek of newness unquestioned,
contentment & pretence in equal measure,
materially expressed & found parked up

in rows, a neat rank that grows
with every hour yet more rank.
the sky is crying daddy, he says,

the sad earth shrinks beneath our feet.
each little word a blunted spear
into the softness of our hearts.

& from the mouths of babes
will always come the steady drip of truth.
so witness this, the march of all

the landless mice, filling our b-roads
with their silent protests. they come
to feed on the scraps of our progress,

to fill their swollen bellies ripe to split,
to celebrate the lessons of an endless
greed; mooted, amended & agreed

at the table of our liberty. tonight,
our cities & our land will once again
be sacked to tame a primal need;

the probing hoard with dark, green eyes
bulging from every mousey head,
will fill their saddle-bags with fool's gold

& leave us to lament its loss.

the sound of it

beanley, northumberland

a stand-off symphony
of posturing cats, a birthing
ewe, a straining hinge,
a sap-bound knot
resisting the screw.

the lurching groan
of ice-bound ships,
an aria of keening gulls,
the snowflake melting
in a scarecrow's breath.

the vacuum melody
of an empty past,
mourning the death
of loss itself.

come where the heather blooms

inkerman pit, tow law, co. durham

burn graphite rain,
spear the sodden earth
of this tumescent fell,
of this crimean fall.

& speak forsaken wind
of ghosts, of young john
graham, of willis, platt
& spark. lost to the vacuum

of an unforgiving dark.
blue metal, seggar clay,
the cavil & the kirve,
the dull lament of straining

props, whose resin weeps
for the broken jud. take stock
my friend, these scars, these
seams are not as they seem;

not brockwell or ballarat
but the black counter-logic
of the thin five quarter.
& two redundant galloways

who daily dream of honey sun,
& breathless gallops 'round
the old mart field, take shelter
from the arctic's ripping claws .

they stand in indian file
behind a bleached out post
that leans against a plangent
sky who's mourned enough

& would that i could paint away
her grief & stake a claim on her behalf,
on all those pretty, diamond stars
in the reverend espin's heaven.

acknowledged land

coalburn, eglingham, northumberland

weep november cold tears,
make this ford impassable.

hide us in the mizzle caul of ancient fears,
protect us from this reiver dark.

fox cry, plangent grace,
the wearing lines

of history on her face:
the ghost of static mines,

the broken ribs of rusted ships,
of shoulders laden with flaccid chips.

inscribe a legend on your map,
no longer whippet & cloth cap

but totem statuary here & there,
a culture raped, the cupboard bare.

this north, this cold, acknowledged land
where rule is cheap & underhand

where heritage is all the rage
& all our rage now heritage.

nightfishing

tynemouth long-sands, north tyneside

moon flecked,
the spectral gulls
in storm flight;
insomniac.

the quiet dreams
of wordless men
a blur in the wheeze
of turbine waves.

our decades of rage,
of toil & the grievous,
buried like mammoths
in this permafrost sand.

& cold-gripped feet
crack the brulee hoar:
a dance-step bequest
of insignia petals .

we read the rod's
convulsive jig;
through swell-surge
& wind-whip,

through kelp-snag
& sand-bar shift,
unravelling patterns
in disjunctive beats.

& then the take. that
codling yank. the strike.
the adrenaline tremor
of the steady retrieve.

a mizzle of tears
jumping like fleas
from the flattened arc
of bow-taut line.

the promise of weight
sculpted in the tip-flex.
a wake in the froth
of surf, the plump

curve of fish, each
tail-flap debossed
on the rabid tide.
the catch is landed.

clouds bear witness.
the night a filigree
of stagnant light
from dying stars.

& flecked by moon,
cadaver blue,
a spectral gull
insomniac.

the sea has left her mark,
fingerprints on the beach,
her ice-kiss legacy
on our fractured lips.

the flying dutchman

church point, newbiggin, northumberland

snow-blind the
ocean squints

the heavy lids
of every break

contracting like
a sphere of hope

& prayers find a cantor
in the southward loons

their scales of absence
sculpted like resolve

in the tide's black lurch.
& rust-blooms flourish

in the shackled knell
of landlocked cobles.

salt

st. mary's island, north tyneside

do clouds dement?
forget their way?

mislay the names of those
they've cast with shadows?

scarce empathy in flood,
each blitzkrieg breaker

exploding with the greyness
of the almost remembered.

i will dance at the wake
of these fragile wrecks,

draw hopeful breaths
from a stowaway's faith.

there is therapy in salt,
in the constancy of tide

spring tide

kitty brewster, blyth, northumberland

feather-weed
& elver weave
in mingling brine.

the fleshless pelt of
a drowned jack russell
upholstering a clutch
of mud-packed pebbles.

& mute, the self
effacing sun lays
down a sediment of
breath-warm shade.

mourner, cruciform;
the casual shag,
a velvet glow of jet.

the glassblower's ghost

seaton sluice, northumberland

the sun is on his honkers,
rendered squat in winter's grip.

blistered, gaunt & photo-fixed,
we catch the blankness of his face:

the broken veins of a bugler's jowl,
eyes glazed with the glare of flame.

he haunts the bulge of imperfect panes,
the lawless curves of slouching bottles;

 his gaze opaque. his smile half-made.
a swarm of promises & well-wrought tales,

trapped in the bubbles of his defunct breath.
through skies as blue as death-filled lips,

we track the flight of lonesome gulls.
the past is not yet done with us.

pen bal crag

tynemouth, north tyneside

cruel illusion. the sun
usurped by nordic cold.

here, stones rot like teeth
& three kings find rest.

broth of crown & bone
melting into salted clay.

the edge of everything.
a trinity of joyous gulls.

we are waving off
departing clouds.

behold this union:
the smiling of eye,

the curious of mouth,
the father & the sons.

liturgy

killingworth, north tyneside

the lake is mute
cold stones
& the liturgy of breath
fracturing its surface

the anderson's youngest
lost to the pond
the reluctant dead's fading glance
haunting the glare of black water

do the dead inhabit the stars?

& poor missus stephenson
of consumptive lungs
drowning in the greyness

inhale

the citadel breached
brutal concrete corroded
someone's dream dismantled
heaped now in garish barrows

round here the streets are damson
percussion in the practised
gobbings of hubba bubba
pale flesh on display
goose bumps & bony arms

the trolleys call like gulls:
white bread
white bread
white bread

the swans are speaking
but we do not have their language
oblivious, pristine communicants
their deferential eyes bowed

repeat after me
we are free
we are free

a swan can break a man's arm
& leda's heart

inhale

a legion of ghosts
words grown cold on their lips
caged
fading like chalk-lines in heavy drizzle

plangent voices
knotted like tatted hair
dissolving like skin

wet earth clutches each footfall
like memory
the cruel legacy of loss
the slow breath of dust settling

inhale

& do the dead inhabit the stars?
do swans strip off their wings
& leave them hidden under a bush?
so that...so that...so that

dark matter
no matter
mad as a hatter
the sky is spilled ink
the killi crew faded in the underpass

its concrete leached
& cancerous
each rusted tumour growing to a fracture
honeycombed, like swan bones

& at prosperous pit
at prospero's pit
ghost horses
conjured from the main seam

& cold tears too
on paradise row
the anxious creak of shale
the groan of basalt bearing down

the poisoned soul
the poisoned soil

a legion of accusing eyes
this site a battlefield
not culloden or dunkirk
but the mire of agincourt
wet earth clutching each foot-fall

inhale

the silent hiss of firedamp
the bark stripped trees
the reebok grins
go west
on scaffold hill
the creaking bough
a bitter moor strangled by the letch

traffic sighs
hissing tyres whisper threats
conversation trapped
growing more distant
with every stuttering beat of the clock

& cat's eye headlights
cut the darkness
a blizzard of mould spores
caught in the strobe

a swan can break a man's heart

inhale

the slow breath of dust settling
of histories lost

& do the dead inherit the stars.

pledge

stonefoot wind farm, co.durham

clouds dance over stonefoot,
the slow song of light & dark,

a chorus of steel flowers reel,
in unison, address the breeze,

the annular swoop & time incites
each petal curve to slice the air

to whisper in the turquoise skies
a simple pledge to dream, to care

breath

sunderland, co. durham

salt-bleached the seagulls spin
& wheel, they strain against this bitter
wind to rake a loose imperfect arc
above the muted autumn hiss

of broken land. precise, the blades
of pristine wings dissect the lime-
washed verdi gris of shrinking days,
of rain-charged skies & in

the convex mirrors of their eyes
a city's tangled narrative unwinds.
an archipelago of lives entwined
by grid-locked lines scratched on a map

by fragile threads, the simple weight
of someone's breath could easily snap.

election day

north shields, north tyneside

half-baked, the day
rests on stolen laurels

& hope is scuffed
like softened leather

hollow men & grey
weak smiles & thin lips

the cut of their faces
a study in blankness

put us to the sword again
feign mercy in our dying

obese, the clouds retaliate
spitting banners of icy shade

& we, the legion of dust & dirt,
collective in the drizzle hiss.

inficete

north shields, north tyneside

laden, the clouds
will charge to greet

the bloodless gnaw
of prodigal cold.

history in the whine
of these futile gulls;

they rage against
the force of gale.

all warmth dissolved,
their flight now stasis.

a misanthrope chokes
on a nugget of sun.

a whole, slow life to learn
the virtue of ambivalence.

union

cullercoats, north tyneside

again un-drowned,
the sand subsides

buckles in the weight
of this keening sky.

sun, mute alchemist,
shadow-smith, gilder,

fashion each footfall
a perfect fitting slipper.

moon-beat & tide-toll,
selkie & breathless salt;

blood bound in bubbling
slicks of summer kelp.

doubt dissolving in the thrash,
in this union of inseparables.

aspic

yeavering bell, northumberland

from up on high
we mutely watch

the epochs burn .
the sea-rats mock

the whispered flames.
blood-lined, our lungs

acquire ancestral ache,
they hiss like swans

their language snared
in drought-bound heather.

from here, our quiet rage
provoked, a universe in aspic

the only measure of distance
now, a slurred vow of time & love

nugget

cowpen, blyth, northumberland

the morning glows
in light's precision

gull flank & vague cloud
swallow curve & birch

their careless arcs
a covenant of grace

a neat blood-knot
of breath & bone

of lore & before
the coalhouse door

today i am here
to say goodbye,

a ferric nugget
in my throat

anatomy

bamburgh, northumberland

we are drawing again
familiar lines, bulging,

gouged like memory
on this routed sand

each stroke wide as faith
every stop deep as defeat

precise & imperfect
the anatomy of rage.

these flags are dead
loyalty anachronous

our lungs collapsed,
our pasts exhaled

each draught of breath
a ghosted incendiary

the diggers

bebside furnace, northumberland

the low sun sober
& us, transported.

vital boys to tired
men. our rhetoric

forged in this cold
fire. crucible, youth

& dreams to slash
the peace of night.

expectant, this clay
is exhumed flesh ;

a century of centuries
dormant. noble & quiet.

anticipates the drag
of our blunted spits.

refrain

north shields, north tyneside

plump blooms stoop,
scorched by the reek

of a sycophant's breath.
we grasp the backward

flow of time; humming
the melody of our decay.

no need now
for crystal balls.

any of these
will do the trick:

a pearl of sweat,
a briny tear,

a prick of blood
that's robbed of red.